O9-AIG-641

NATIONAL
GEOGRAPHIC
KiDS

Master-Mind

Over **100** GAMES, TESTS, and PUZZLES to Unleash Your Inner Genius

Stephanie Warren Drimmer

with puzzles by
Julie K. Cohen

NATIONAL GEOGRAPHIC

WASHINGTON, D.C.

Contents

CHAPTER ONE

Meet the Mastermind

IMA GENIUS
CERTIFIED MASTERMIND

Greetings, average human.

My name is Ima Genius, and I'm a certified Mastermind and your host for this book. Want to become one, too? Ha—good luck! Why, I bet you don't even know the first thing about that magical, marvelous organ inside your skull! For example, did you know that a brain creates 70,000 thoughts per day? And that's just the average thinker! My own noggin probably pumps out twice that many, at least!

I'm a regular know-it-all and proud of it. I'm a fact freak, an academic ace, a numbers nerd! Masterminds like me are few and far between, and that's just not good for the future of humankind. That's where you come in. Just this once, I'm willing to share all of the knowledge in my superior skull with one lucky beginner brain—yours. I'll be your guide to the inside of your own head. I'll wow you with strange science and dazzle you with freaky facts.

While I'm doing it, I'll be your mental trainer. My games and puzzles will turn your couch potato brain into a heavy-weight champ. When I'm finished with you, your brain will be so huge that your average-size neck will no longer be able to support your massive noggin. Ha! I kid. That's only happened once.

In exchange for all my hard work, all I ask is that you take the quiz at the end of each chapter. These experimen— Uh, I mean, fun questions, will let me peer inside your brain and see how it works.

Only once you have completed all the quizzes will you be a certified Master-mind. After that, I'll harness the power of your exceptional brain to take over the worl— Err, never mind. Let's get started!

Ima Genius

P.S. We can't forget about my loyal lab assistant, Atom. Atom is no doggy dummy— with a few simple experiments, I've made him a canine cranial champion! Watch for him in these pages—he'll be telling you about animals with amazing abilities. Just don't show him a tennis ball—he gets a little distracted.

FUN FACT
Your brain generates enough electricity to power a lightbulb.

ATOM
CANINE CRANIAL CHAMPION

Making the Most of Mastermind

I'M SURE IF YOU'VE MADE IT THIS FAR YOU KNOW HOW A *NORMAL* BOOK WORKS: TURN THE PAGE, READ THE WORDS, REPEAT.

But *Mastermind* is no ordinary book! There are key features, tips, tricks, and trials you'll want to be sure you don't skip along the way!

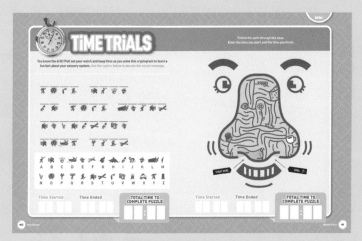

Time Trials

There are two of these speedster tests in every chapter. Set a timer, and then—ready, set, GO!—solve the puzzles as quickly as you can. If you get faster each time, it means the workouts are working to beef up your brain!

Tips and Tricks

Look for the magnifying glass for helpful hints in case you get stuck. Also, from time to time Atom or I might pop up to fill you in on some important info, so be sure to hang on my every word. Ha! As if you could tear yourself away ...

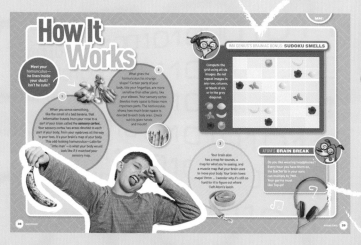

Brainiac Bonuses and Brain Breaks!

Watch out for Brainiac Bonus puzzles on your journey to Mastermind status—they might throw you for a loop! And a beginner brain such as yours might need a rest every now and then, so be on the lookout for Atom—he likes to share silly-but-true Brain Breaks.

Myths Busted!

Along the road to mind molding, look for Myths Busted! to discover why the truth is not always as it seems. Some things you've thought were true all your life might be big ol' whoppers!

Mastermind Meter!

Can't feel your brain bulging quite yet? Have no fear, my dear! I've included a handy Mastermind Meter at the end of each chapter, so you can see how your brain is growing right before your eyes.

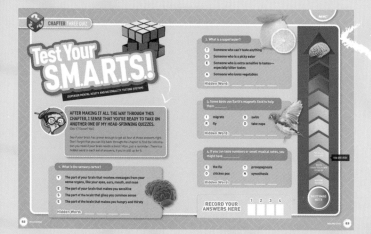

To weed out the budding brainiacs from the smarty-pants superstars, I've moved the answer section all the way to the back of the book to ensure there's no cheating in this cranium competition. But don't feel too bad if you get stumped every now and then and have to visit the answer section. Even geniuses aren't right 100 percent of the time—aside from me, of course. Just follow the Mastermind code of honor and vow to try it on your own before you wave the white flag.

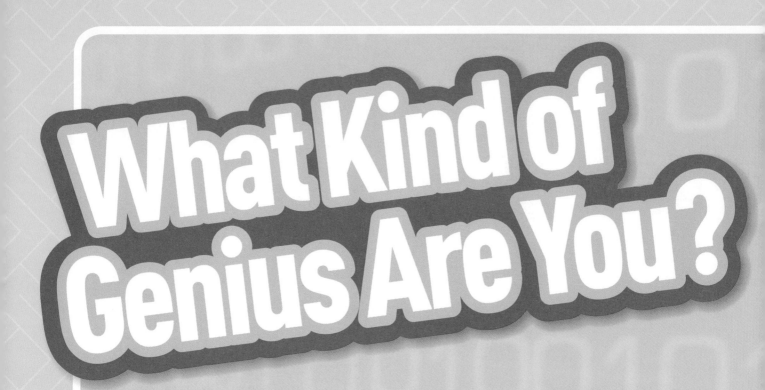

What Kind of Genius Are You?

OH, YOU'RE STILL HERE. I GUESS YOU REALLY *DO* WANT TO BE A MASTERMIND, HUH? Well, before I start whipping your piddling brain into shape, I'd better see what I'm working with.

Take the quiz on the next page to discover what kind of genius you are ... then look for your Genius Genus throughout the book to see which puzzles are right up your alley!

1. You can't find your favorite "Dinosaurs Were Dino-Mite!" sweatshirt. To track it down, you start by:

A. Making a mental checklist of where you could have left it: your closet, the laundry room, your soccer bag.

B. Closing your eyes and imagining where you were when you were last wearing it.

C. Talking to your mom about it. Sometimes chatting about a problem sparks your memory.

D. Opening your drawers and looking at your other clothes. "Let's see, last time I wore the sweatshirt, I was wearing those pants and that hat ... That was on Monday ... I know! I left it at my piano lesson!"

2. Your toughest teacher, Ms. Meanie, assigned you a big book project due in two weeks. Here's how you tackle it:

A. You break down the project into steps. First you write up an outline. Then you pull out the calendar and assign those steps to dates. All you have to do is follow your plan and you're set.

B. You grab a piece of paper and your colored pencils and start scribbling. You draw a mind map connecting all the parts of the book you want to talk about in your project.

C. Easy peasy! Your favorite parts of the book are crystal clear in your memory. You just have to list them and go from there.

D. You can't think of anything to write about for a week. Then inspiration strikes! You're lying in bed one night when the ideas start flowing. You grab a pen and quickly jot them down!

3. You're babysitting, and the kid is driving you nuts! If you don't think of a way to entertain him—quickly—he's going to start coloring on the walls. You:

A. Reason with him. If he behaves, you'll let him watch the latest superhero movie—even though you've already seen it.

B. Grab a pen and paper—you're going to create a treasure map that will send him on a search through the house for his favorite candy.

C. Tell him a story. Once upon a time, there was a prince and a scary, fire-breathing dragon ...

D. Look around the room for inspiration. There's a pack of rubber bands on the desk—bingo! Catapult contest time.

4. The science fair is coming up, and this year, you're going to win. Here's how you figure out a topic:

A. You make a list of problems you've been having lately: Your shoes come untied all the time, your bookmark keeps slipping out of your novel. Invent a solution, and you've got a blue ribbon winner!

B. You start doodling: There's you with your backpack and headphones on ... Hey, what if your backpack had a solar panel that could charge your iPod?

C. You hear the TV in the background—it's the weather report. That makes you wonder: Why does my nose run when it's cold outside? Bingo! You've got your topic!

D. You go for a walk to clear your head. You're circling the park when—out of nowhere—an idea comes to you. You grab your notepad and sketch out your plans for Robo-Chef, a robot that makes you pancakes while you sleep in.

MOSTLY As

LOGICAL LEADER
MARIE CURIE

You're a Logical Leader. Your brain is good at exploring cause-and-effect relationships and finding patterns. You like to do experiments, solve puzzles, and investigate mysteries. You like logic games and math.

Marie Curie was a chemist who lived from 1867 to 1934. She is famous for her experiments that helped discover **radioactivity**—which is what happens when elements spontaneously emit energy (it's what powers X-ray machines that can see through your skin!). She was the first person to win two Nobel Prizes for her work. Now that's some genius girl power!

LOOK FOR

GENIUS GENUS:
LOGICAL LEADER

MOSTLY Bs

SPATIAL SUPERSTAR
ALBERT EINSTEIN

You are a Spatial Superstar. You like to think in pictures, and you're good at drawing, jigsaw puzzles, charts, graphs, and reading maps.

Albert Einstein was a physicist who lived from 1879 to 1955. He is most famous for thinking up the theory of **general relativity,** which explains how planets in outer space orbit each other. Einstein was known for being able to come up with complex mathematical theories by just visualizing how objects move in space!

LOOK FOR

GENIUS GENUS:
SPATIAL SUPERSTAR

MOSTLY Cs

WORD WIZARD
WILLIAM SHAKESPEARE

You are a Word Wizard. You love language and everything about it. You like words and reading, and you're excellent at word games, such as rhyming, crossword puzzles, and word searches.

William Shakespeare was a writer who lived from 1564 to 1616. Shakespeare was such a witty wordsmith that the English language wasn't enough for him—when he needed a phrase that didn't exist yet, he would invent one. Without him, we wouldn't say things like "Wild goose chase," "Dead as a doornail," or even "Knock, knock—who's there?"

W₄ O₁ R₁ D₂

LOOK FOR → GENIUS GENUS: WORD WIZARD

MOSTLY Ds

CREATIVITY CHAMPION
LEONARDO DA VINCI

You are a Creativity Champion, and you're great at thinking outside the box. People look to your brain when it comes to problems that require that "aha!" moment to solve—such as riddles. Your best work comes in moments of inspiration.

Leonardo da Vinci, who lived from 1452 to 1519, was a painter, sculptor, architect, musician, writer, engineer ... and the list goes on. He painted one of the most famous paintings in the world, the "Mona Lisa," and in his spare time he created plans for flying machines, an armored vehicle, and solar power, just to name a few. This guy was good at everything!

GENIUS GENUS: CREATIVITY CHAMPION ← LOOK FOR

Brain Basics

IF WE WERE TO CUT OPEN YOUR SKULL RIGHT NOW, WHAT WOULD WE SEE? NOT THAT I'VE EVER DONE THAT BEFORE. I'VE JUST, UM, SEEN PICTURES ...

Here's the harsh truth: If you could see your brain up close, you might be a little disappointed. Don't take it personally—even my own magnificent melon isn't much to look at. A brain is a pale pink lump that weighs about three pounds (1.4 kg). If you reached out and poked it, it would be spongy and slimy and ... well, kind of gross.

So your brain isn't ever going to win a beauty pageant. But it's still pretty special. Let me ask you a question: What is the most powerful machine in the universe? Think about it: maybe a supercomputer? Psht, not even close! Consider this: In 2013, a team of scientists did something amazing. Using 82,000 processors from one of the most powerful super-computers in the world, they were able to generate enough thinking power to equal ... one percent of the activity of a human brain, for one single second.

Scientists have built rockets that can shoot people more than 250,000 miles (402,336 km) into outer space and land them precisely on the moon. But they aren't even close to creating a device that matches the power of the human brain. Now *that's* a marvelous machine!

AVERAGE WEIGHT: ABOUT 3 POUNDS (1.4 KG)

Your brain has 86 billion **neurons**, or nerve cells. They're all linked together, making trillions of different connections. To talk to each other, these neurons use the power of electricity. That's right, the same thing that cooks your toaster waffles! Talk about brilliant!

Every moment (even when you're sleeping!) countless electrical signals are zipping around your head, skipping from neuron to neuron, all at the same time.

Using our incredible brainpower, we've built cities, sent people into space, and even figured out how the universe began. But there's one mystery we still haven't been able to solve: how our own brains work! How does that squishy pink lump of flesh create your thoughts and feelings, memories, hopes, even love?

FUN FACT

Neurons send info to your brain at more than 150 miles an hour (241 km/h).

Brain Basics

Right now, scientists all over the world are working to solve the secrets of the human brain. In these pages, you'll find a little of what they've already discovered.

Look back at your quiz results. Are you a Word Wizard? Your brain's Broca's and Wernicke's areas (more on these in chapter 7) are in tip-top shape. A Logical Leader? Your frontal cortex (coming up again in chapter 9) is buff. But don't limit yourself! The most amazing thing about the human brain is that the more you use it, the stronger it gets. So it's time to hit the mental gym and bulk up that pip-squeak thinker of yours!

Big Brain

The award for Earth's Biggest Brain goes to ... the sperm whale! Its thunderous thinker clocks in at 18 pounds (8.2 kg). But if we were to shrink a sperm whale down to human size, its brain would look teeny-tiny next to ours. In fact, if all animals on Earth were the same size, humans would have the biggest brains of all.

Having a big brain is a pretty big deal. I don't mean to sound big-headed (get it?!)—it's just the facts! That's because brains are like jet planes—they need a lot of fuel to run. Even though your brain makes up just 2 percent of your body weight, it uses a whopping 20 percent of your body's energy! Kind of selfish, huh?

Two Sides

Each side of your brain controls one half of your body. But the sides are swapped: The right side of your brain controls the left side of your body, and vice versa. Nobody knows why for sure—how twisted!

Each side of your brain has different strengths. For example, the left side is better at counting, whereas the right side is better at reading emotions. The two sides of your brain have to work together to solve problems. So get along, you two!

LEFT SIDE   RIGHT SIDE

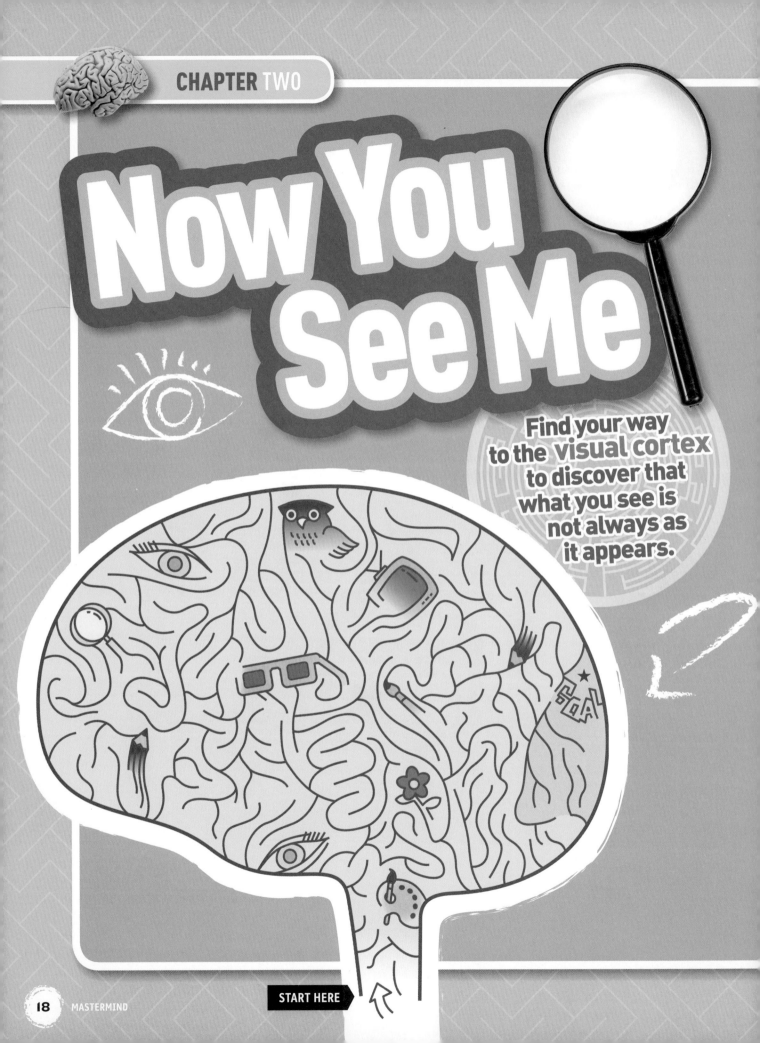

CHAPTER TWO

Now You See Me

Find your way to the **visual cortex** to discover that what you see is not always as it appears.

START HERE

OK, student, listen up. If we're going to turn your puny brain into a blue ribbon champion of thought, you need to know a little secret: Every time you open your eyes, your brain lies to you.

I know what you're thinking, your brain would never do such a thing! But in reality, it has no choice. See, your brain can't process every single teensy-weensy detail of everything your eyes are seeing. So it guesses, filling in the blanks with whatever it thinks should be there. All without you knowing—how sneaky!

Sometimes, your brain's visual center makes mistakes. (Want proof? Check out the optical illusions on pages 30-31!) But usually, it does a pretty good job. That's because one-third of your brain is devoted to vision. That's hundreds of millions of neurons—more than it uses for all your other senses combined! Want to see how it works? (Get it? I'm so clever!) Read on!

How It Works

1

Light enters your eye through a tiny hole called the **pupil.**

2

Your **lens** focuses the light onto the back of your eye, which is covered with cells called **photoreceptors.** They work like translators, changing the light into electrical signals—the language of your brain.

These electrical signals travel down the **optic nerve** to the brain. There, the brain uses them to create a mental picture of your world.

3

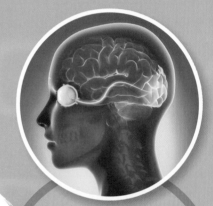

See for Yourself

Did you know that your pupils change size? Standing in front of a mirror, close your eyes for a few seconds. Then open them, and watch your pupils expand as conditions change from dark to light.

ATOM'S **BRAIN BREAK**

It's impossible for most people to lick their own elbow. (But something tells me you're trying it now. Silly human.)

MYTHS
BUSTED!

MYTH: When Columbus set sail, people thought the world was flat. He could have gone right over the edge!

BUSTED!: People have known Earth is a sphere since the ancient Greeks figured it out in the 3rd century B.C. They had lots of clues to go on—for example, when a ship is on the horizon, its lower part is hidden by Earth's curves.

TiME TRiALS

Are you ready for your first Time Trial? Grab a pencil, and make sure you have a clock handy. Write down your start and end times to figure out how long it took you. Throughout this book, you may notice that you're getting speedier at solving these puzzles!

Can you see the hidden message?
Use the cypher below to decode the secret message.

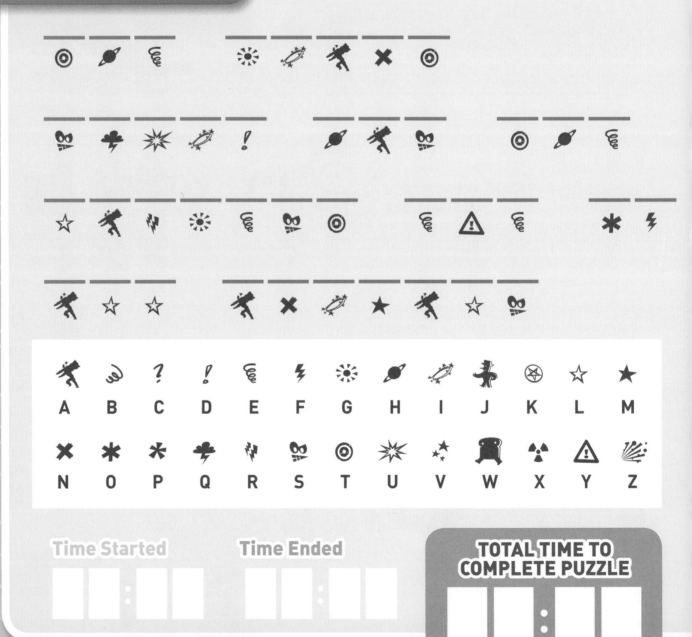

Time Started

Time Ended

TOTAL TIME TO COMPLETE PUZZLE

Find your way to the pupil. Don't forget to enter
the time you start and the time you finish.

START HERE

Time Started

Time Ended

**TOTAL TIME TO
COMPLETE PUZZLE**

Super Sight!

YOU HUMANS THINK YOUR EYES ARE SO EXTRAORDINARY—HA! It's true that when it comes to optical excellence, I'm far from top dog: I can't even see the color red. But these four animals are true visual virtuosos!

EYE IN THE SKY

Ever call someone with super-sharp vision an "eagle eye"? (Perhaps that teacher who always catches you passing a note?) Well, it's for good reason. Eagles hunt for small animals from high in the sky. To do that, they need super-duper eyesight—eagles can spot a rabbit on the ground from two miles (3.2 km) away!

Humans have just one **fovea,** or focusing spot, on the back of their eyes; eagles have two: one for forward vision and one for sideways vision. Using both foveae together, an eagle can see nearly all the way around itself—340 degrees—without turning its head. What a fortunate fowl!

FUNFACT
If you had the vision of an eagle, you could spot an ant on the ground from the top of a ten-story building!

THIRD-EYE KIND

When you think of creatures with three eyes, visions of aliens from distant planets probably pop into your brain. Not so fast, simple two-eyed human. Three-eyed creatures are actually all around. Lizards have a small spot on the top of their heads called the **parietal eye** that works like a third eye. Scientists think that these crafty crawlers use it as a compass—it keeps an "eye" on the position of the sun to help the lizards find their way around.

A SCORPION OF A DIFFERENT COLOR

Did you know that your eyes only see three different colors? That's it. Just red, blue, and yellow. Every other color you see—from green to hot pink to turquoise—is made of combinations of these three colors. Pretty cool, huh?

Some animals, such as dogs, only see two colors. Others, like jumping spiders, see four—meaning they see a whole range of colors that we can't even imagine. This range is called the **ultraviolet** spectrum, and seeing it gives the spiders one really cool superpower—they can spot prey in the dark. For example, to humans, the black emperor scorpion is completely hidden at night. But to jumping spiders, it glows bright green! Talk about a fluorescent feast!

SLY EYE

The cuttlefish can't see color, but make no mistake, this ocean dweller has some of the sharpest eyes in the animal kingdom. Cuttlefish can see a special kind of light called **polarized light** that human eyes can't detect.

Cuttlefish not only see polarized light, they also use it like a secret language! These crafty creatures can alter the patterns on their bodies to communicate. By using polarized light to change their outfits, cuttlefish can send secret signals that only other cuttlefish can see. Now that's a sneaky sense!

Are You Color Blind?

The most common type of color blindness is red-green color blindness. About 7 percent of men have this type of color blindness. In women, color blindness is very rare. Are you color blind? Find out with this test:

Try to find a circle, star, and square in the image below.

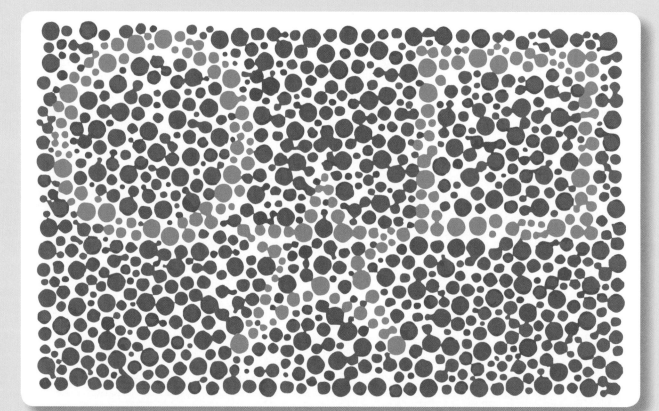

Wow, those animals on the last page have some incredible eyes! Don't worry, yours aren't so bad, either. Why don't you solve these vision puzzles to prove it?

Dog Vision

GENIUS GENUS: CREATIVITY CHAMPION

Have you ever wondered how your dog sees the world? The picture on the top shows a scene as a human would see it. The picture on the bottom shows the same scene as a dog would see it. Can you find all ten objects in each picture? Was it more difficult with human vision or dog vision?

FIND ME:
1. fire hydrant
2. red pail
3. beach ball
4. basketball
5. flowerpot
6. cardinal
7. bunch of balloons
8. flags
9. red starfish
10. blue sand pail

The Man Who Didn't Know His Own Face

IMAGINE COMING TO THE KITCHEN IN THE MORNING ONLY TO FIND A STRANGER MAKING YOU BREAKFAST. You head outside to the neighborhood you've lived in all your life, and you don't recognize any of the people mowing their lawns or walking their dogs. And when you look at your reflection in the mirror—surprise!—you see someone you've never met.

That's what life is like for people with a condition called face blindness, or **prosopagnosia.** Normally, people are very good at recognizing faces. In fact, the human brain has a special area devoted only to this task! The human brain is wired to be a face-spotting genius, because faces are how we figure out the emotions of people around us. People with face blindness don't have this skill because this area of their brain is damaged.

The most famous person with face blindness is nicknamed Dr. P. He is a teacher, a gifted musician, and a very intelligent man. But his condition makes him do quirky things. He often doesn't recognize his own students. Sometimes, when walking down the street, he pats the tops of parking meters, thinking they are children's heads. And once, in a doctor's office, he tried to grab his wife's head, lift it up, and put it on—he thought it was his hat! Now that's what you call a case of mistaken identity!

IMA GENIUS'S BRAINIAC BONUS: **WORD LADDER**

Transform BRAIN into CRAWL. You may only change one letter on each row, and each change must result in a new word. Complete the transformation in four moves or less.

B	R	A	I	N
C	R	A	W	L

Perplexing Perceptions

The visual center of your brain is divided into different sections. Each helps you see something specific. One is responsible for color vision, one sees shapes, another recognizes faces, and so on.

People with damage to these areas experience strange visual effects. One woman had damage to the area of her brain that sees motion. When she looked at a car moving down the street, she saw the scene as a series of snapshots: First the car was by the stop sign, then by the yellow house, then by the mailbox. When she poured water from a pitcher, the stream of water looked like a column of clear glass. She couldn't see how fast her cup was filling up, so she always poured water onto the table!

All right, Mastermind-in-training, it's time to get serious about whipping that weak little brain into shape! Check out my eye-bending illusions. Will your meager mind be fooled?

Flower Power

Stare at the center of the flower on the left for 15 seconds.
Then stare at the black dot on the right. What do you see?

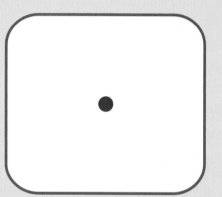

Blind Spot

Everybody has a blind spot in each eye. Take this test to see for yourself!
Look at the graphic above with your nose pointing between the cross and the circle. Cover your LEFT eye and stare at the cross with your RIGHT eye. Now *slowly* move your face toward the page while still staring at the cross with your RIGHT eye. As you move closer to the page, the circle will disappear. The circle is in your **blind spot.** Now try the other eye. Cover your RIGHT eye this time and stare at the circle with your LEFT eye. Move closer to make the cross disappear.

Tricky Lines

Which line is the longest?

What Is It?

1

2

3

1. What is this shape? When you think you know, continue to step 2.

2. Turn the book counterclockwise, so the 2 is at the top. Do you see a different image?

3. Now turn the book counterclockwise again, so the 3 is at the top, and you will see one more image.

Face It

Notice anything strange about this picture? Turn the book upside down.

Anything amiss now? This frightening face phenomenon is called the Thatcher Effect. Scientists aren't sure why it happens, but they think it has to do with the brain's special ability to perceive faces. The Thatcher Effect doesn't work on people with some forms of face blindness—they notice that the features are facing the wrong way before they see the image right-side up.

Illusive X

GENIUS GENUS: SPATIAL SUPERSTAR

For this challenge, you may either draw your solution or build it using eight half circles you have cut from scrap paper. The half circles you draw or cut out may be smaller or larger that those used here, as long as they are equal in size to one another.

The Challenge: Rearrange the eight half circles to create an X.

Eye See the Answer

Complete the puzzle from the word list below

GENIUS GENUS: WORD WIZARD

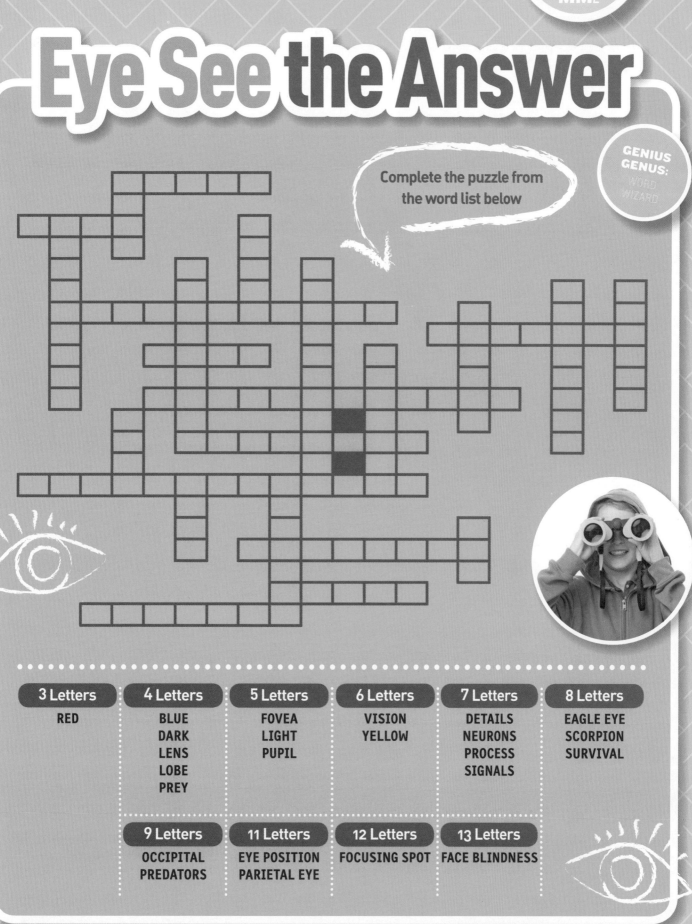

3 Letters	4 Letters	5 Letters	6 Letters	7 Letters	8 Letters
RED	BLUE	FOVEA	VISION	DETAILS	EAGLE EYE
	DARK	LIGHT	YELLOW	NEURONS	SCORPION
	LENS	PUPIL		PROCESS	SURVIVAL
	LOBE			SIGNALS	
	PREY				

9 Letters	11 Letters	12 Letters	13 Letters
OCCIPITAL	EYE POSITION	FOCUSING SPOT	FACE BLINDNESS
PREDATORS	PARIETAL EYE		

Test Your S.M.A.R.T.S.!

(SUPERIOR MENTAL ACUITY AND RATIONALITY TESTING SYSTEM)

WELL, WELL, WELL ... I NEVER THOUGHT YOU'D MAKE IT PAST THOSE VISUALLY VICIOUS PUZZLES, BUT I GUESS I WAS WRONG. Maybe your pea brain does have some potential after all. Let's find out, shall we? Use what you've learned in this chapter to answer the following questions. Each answer choice is labeled with a letter. When you finish the quiz, write each question's answer (just the circled letter) in the blue answer box. I'll give you a big hint: You'll need them later. I won't tell you why, because, well, what fun would that be?

Oh—and if you're feeling particularly brainy today, feel free to tackle my bonus challenge and find the hidden word for each question. Here's a clue: Unscramble each answer's four circled letters to find a key word. Good luck—you'll need it!

1. What do the photoreceptors in your eyes do?

K Tell your eyes which direction to look

O Focus light onto the back of your eyes

L Translate light entering your eyes into the electrical signals that the brain can understand

O Take photos each time you blink

Hidden Word: ___ ___ ___ ___

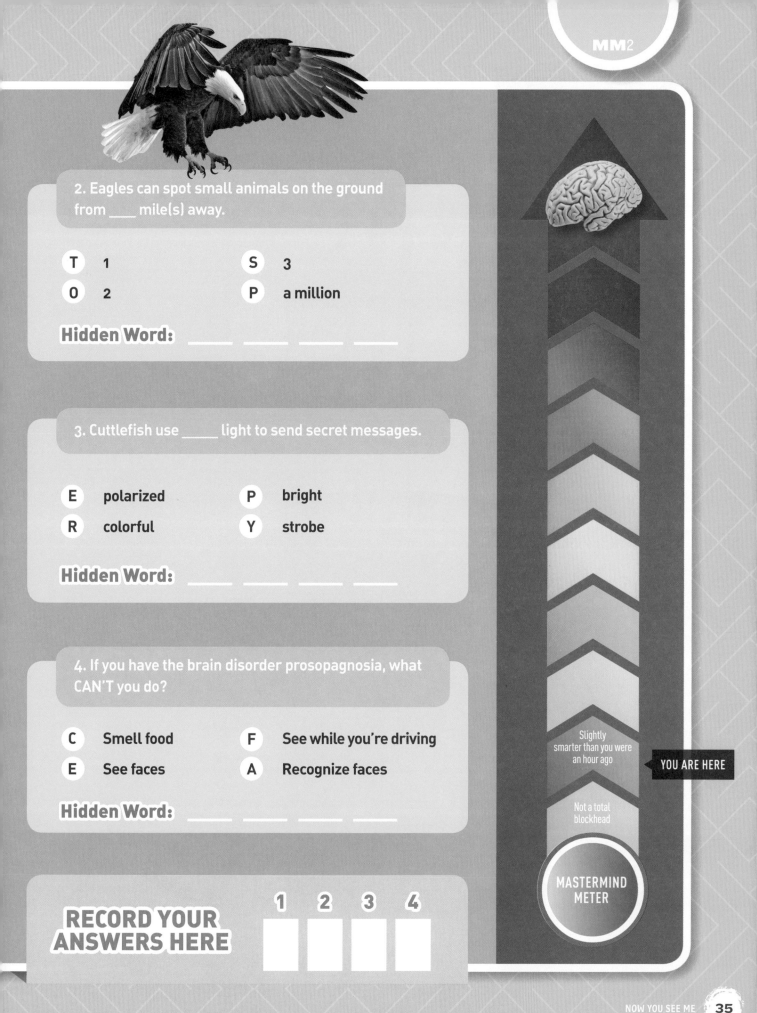

2. Eagles can spot small animals on the ground from _____ mile(s) away.

T 1	**S** 3
O 2	**P** a million

Hidden Word: _____ _____ _____ _____

3. Cuttlefish use _____ light to send secret messages.

E polarized	**P** bright
R colorful	**Y** strobe

Hidden Word: _____ _____ _____ _____

4. If you have the brain disorder prosopagnosia, what CAN'T you do?

C Smell food	**F** See while you're driving
E See faces	**A** Recognize faces

Hidden Word: _____ _____ _____ _____

RECORD YOUR ANSWERS HERE

1	2	3	4

Slightly smarter than you were an hour ago

YOU ARE HERE

Not a total blockhead

MASTERMIND METER

CHAPTER THREE

Making Sense

Taste, smell, or touch your way to the sensory cortex.

START HERE

Imagine waking up tomorrow without your senses of taste, smell, or touch. You roll out of bed and head downstairs to breakfast. Pancakes—your favorite! You try to pick up your fork to dig in—but it's nearly impossible with no feeling in your fingers. You finally manage a bite— gross! It's like eating sponges. Maybe maple syrup will help. You take a whiff—but it's just odorless goop. Eww!

You hardly ever think about your senses of taste, smell, and touch, but you use them all the time. You may be no more than a greenhorn at solving my genius games, but even I will admit that when it comes to your senses, you were born an expert! Read on to learn how to bump your senses smarts into Master-mind territory.

How It Works

Meet your homunculus—he lives inside your skull! Isn't he cute?

1

When you sense something, like the smell of a bad banana, that information travels from your nose to a part of your brain called the **sensory cortex.** Your sensory cortex has areas devoted to each part of your body, from your eyebrows all the way to your toes. It's your brain's map of your body. This odd-looking homunculus—Latin for "little man"—is what your body would look like if it matched your sensory map.

2

What gives the homunculus his strange shape? Certain parts of your body, like your fingertips, are more sensitive than other parts, like your elbows. Your sensory cortex devotes more space to these more important parts. The homunculus shows how much brain space is devoted to each body area. Check out his giant hands and mouth!

IMA GENIUS'S BRAINIAC BONUS: **SUDOKU SMELLS**

Complete the grid using all six images. Do not repeat images in any row, column, or block of six, or in the grey diagonal.

3

Your brain also has a map for sounds, a map for what you're seeing, and a muscle map that your brain uses to move your body. Your brain loves maps! Hmm ... I wonder why it's still so hard for it to figure out where I left Atom's leash.

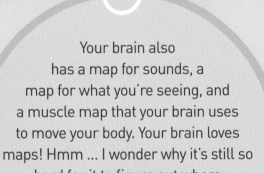

ATOM'S **BRAIN BREAK**

Do you like wearing headphones? Every hour you have them on, the **bacteria** in your ears can multiply by **700.** Your germs must like Top 40!

You know the drill! Pull out your watch and keep time as you solve this cryptogram to learn a fun fact about your sensory system. Use the cypher below to decode the secret message.

A	B	C	D	E	F	G	H	I	J	K	L	M
N	O	P	Q	R	S	T	U	V	W	X	Y	Z

Time Started

☐ ☐ : ☐ ☐ ☐

Time Ended

☐ ☐ : ☐ ☐ ☐

TOTAL TIME TO COMPLETE PUZZLE

☐ ☐ : ☐ ☐

Follow the path through the nose.
Enter the time you start and the time you finish.

START HERE

GOAL ★

Time Started

Time Ended

TOTAL TIME TO COMPLETE PUZZLE

Secret Senses

shhhhh!

HOW MANY SENSES DO YOU HAVE? Did you say five? Ha—fooled you! Besides the standard sight, hearing, touch, taste, and smell, you also have secret senses—ones that you don't even know about! Don't believe me? **Check out these hidden abilities:**

shhhhh!

FUNFACT

You shed and regrow new taste buds about every two weeks.

shhhhh!

SMELL OUT A FRIEND

Your nose is good for more than just smelling when the pizza delivery guy has arrived. You also use it to sniff out people's personalities—without even knowing it!

Think back to when you met your best friend. Did you like him or her right away? All of us get first impressions about people, gut feelings that tell us others are friendly or that we should stay away. These first impressions may have something to do with the way people smell.

Scientists discovered this by asking people to wear the same shirt for three days straight. Afterward, they asked another group to smell the shirts. Phew—I hope they knew what they'd signed up for! The smellers were surprisingly good at guessing how outgoing, anxious, or dominant the shirt wearers were—just from their odor. Now that's some stinky science!

MAGNETIC MELON

Some kinds of birds **migrate,** traveling up and down the globe to stay one step ahead of chilly weather. They find their way across vast distances: The arctic tern can travel 50,000 miles (80,467 km) in a year. But have you ever seen a bird with GPS? No way! So how do they know where to go?

Birds and other migrating animals can sense the magnetic field that encircles Earth by using special cells in their eyeballs. The magnetic field is like a compass that guides their way.

Scientists recently discovered that humans may have these cells, too. No, you can't see magnetic fields. But this extra sense could help us figure out how things move through time and space in a way we don't understand (yet!).

SUPERTASTER

Do you hate broccoli, kale, and brussels sprouts? Your mom might call you a picky eater, but there could be another name for you: supertaster. To about one in four people, foods (especially bitter ones) taste much more intense than they do to the average person.

How do supertasters get their super ability? They have extra **fungiform papillae,** those little bumps on the surface of the tongue. Think you're a supertaster? Too bad—you still have to eat your vegetables!

Migration Mess

GENIUS GENUS: LOGICAL LEADER

Four groups of birds are migrating for the winter. When they left Missouri, a strange storm affected the special cells in their eyes. Now the birds are confused. They need your help to find their way home. Which group of birds belongs in each of the four states below? Here are some clues to help you discover their destinations:

1. **Red Birds** hate anything new.
2. **Green Birds** will live in any state with the letter "O."
3. **Blue Birds** live in a state with two words.
4. **Green Birds** and **Red Birds** don't have neighbors.
5. **Orange birds** aren't picky about where they live.

OREGON

NEW YORK

NEW MEXICO

TEXAS

FUNFACT
More than 300 species of birds migrate to warmer places each year.

Find Your Way

After you solve the crossword, unscramble the yellow squares to solve the bonus question.

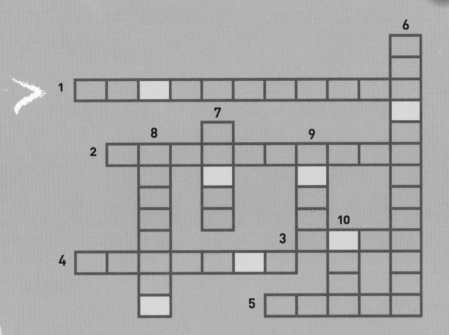

ACROSS

1. If you have extra fungiform papillae, you are a _____.

2. A secret sense may be what gives us our first _____ about people.

3. Without their natural "GPS," migratory animals would become _____.

4. To a person who is a (#1 Across), foods taste more _____.

5. Arctic terns are _____.

DOWN

6. We unknowingly use our noses to sniff peoples' _____.

7. The sensory cortex is found here.

8. A special _____ field encircles Earth, helping some animals navigate.

9. Our standard senses include sight, touch, taste, hearing, and _____.

10. _____ from a person may reveal if he is anxious or outgoing.

BONUS QUESTION

What may help you find your way?

_____

My lab results show that you will be a Mastermind in no time.

Swapped Senses

WHEN FRANCESCA CLOSES HER EYES AND TOUCHES DIFFERENT MATERIALS, SHE FEELS DIFFERENT EMOTIONS.
Stroking silk makes her feel happy and relaxed. Touching a candle makes her feel embarrassed. Rubbing her jeans makes her very sad. Francesca isn't making this up. She has a rare condition called **synesthesia**.

People with synesthesia have connections in their brains that the rest of us don't. Francesca's brain makes a connection between how she feels and what she's touching.

Synesthesia has different effects in different people. One person might see each number as a different color. To that person, a phone number may look like a rainbow! Another person sees orange when she hears C-sharp played on the piano. To her, the piano keys are color coded! Others experience certain tastes when they hear words: To them, the word "socks" might taste like doughnuts. That would get anyone to do the laundry!

Millions of people have synesthesia. Many famous artists and musicians may have had synesthesia, from Vincent van Gogh to Kanye West.

Silly Sounds

Check out the picture on the right. One of these shapes is called Bouba and the other is called Kiki. Which do you think is which?

Did you say that the rounded shape is probably the Bouba and the pointy one Kiki? If so, you're very average. No offense! When scientists gave this test to a group of people, nearly 100 percent answered that same way.

"Bouba" and "Kiki" are nonsense words that the scientists made up! They have nothing to do with the shapes ... or do they?

Scientists think that people may answer the question this way because the roundness of the Bouba shape mimics the rounded shape your mouth makes when you say "booo-baaa." And the sharpness of the Kiki shape mimics the way your tongue snaps against the roof of your mouth when you say "kee-kee."

Bouba and Kiki show us that the names we give objects might not be totally random. Perhaps people with synesthesia aren't so special after all: Maybe all brains make connections between different senses.

MYTH: Humans have five senses.

BUSTED!: Depending on who you ask, humans could have as few as three senses or more than a thousand. The truth is that scientists have not agreed on what is considered a sense. The traditional ones are touch, taste, smell, hearing, and sight. But what about the sense of pain or the sense of balance? There's a lot more to humans than can be categorized five ways!

GENIUS
GENUS:
CREATIVITY
CHAMPION

License Plates

Four drivers need those special cells in their eyes that migratory birds have, because they are lost. They can't even find their own cars in the parking lot! Match the license plates to the drivers.

STATE

FUN-G-4M

STATE

O-DOOR

STATE

MY-GR8

STATE

HMN-Q-LS

BIRD LOVER

TONGUE DOCTOR

BRAIN DOCTOR

GARBAGE COLLECTOR

Use your noggin to knock out this brain buster!

Touch Test

Are your lips more sensitive than your fingertips? What about your kneecaps, your shins, and your toes? All over your skin, you have pressure sensors. Some areas have a lot, others not so many. The more pressure sensors an area has, the more sensitive it is. Find out how sensitive you are with this experiment.

YOU WILL NEED

A PAPER CLIP

A RULER

A PEN AND PAPER

A FRIEND

(You can also try this on your own—just shut your eyes.)

INSTRUCTIONS:

1. Straighten out a paper clip and bend it into a U-shape. Make sure the tips are level with each other and about a half inch (1 cm) apart.

2. Ask a friend to close his or her eyes. Touch both ends of the paper clip gently (and at the same time) onto the back of your friend's hand. Ask if your friend felt one point or two.

3. At sensitive areas of the body, the pressure points are close together. They will detect both points. The less sensitive the area, the farther away the paper clip points will have to be for your friend to feel both of them.

4. If your friend felt only one pressure point, spread the tips of the paper clip and try again. Write down the distance where your friend goes from feeling one pressure point to feeling two pressure points.

5. Be tricky and make it difficult for your friend to guess the answer: Vary the distance between the tips, and sometimes use one point, sometimes both.

TEST THESE BODY PARTS!

Test the palm and back of the hand, fingertips, forearm, upper arm, shoulder, back, neck, cheek, forehead, lips, nose, legs, tips of the toes, and the soles and upper parts of your feet. Which can detect two points with the smallest tip separation? This is the most sensitive part of your body.

Braille Code

Louis Braille developed the braille alphabet for people who can't see. Since your fingers are sensitive enough to tell how many dots are in a small area and what order they are in, you can read different letters simply by touching raised bumps on paper! Here, since the dots are flat, use your eyes instead of your fingers to decode the message below.

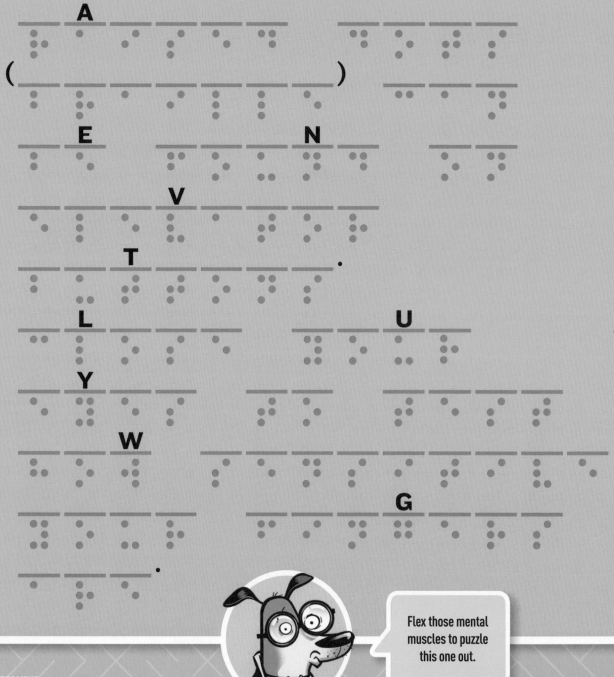

Flex those mental muscles to puzzle this one out.

Touchy Topic

GENIUS GENUS: WORD WIZARD

The words in this search all have something in common.
Once you find the words (which may appear forward,
backward, up, down, and diagonally), you will find your answer.

```
Y   M   I   L   S   S
R   E   C   E   P   O
T   C   O   L   D   F
H   O   R   B   S   T
A   R   O   U   G   H
R   I   N   M   T   T
D   P   W   P   O   O
Y   E   R   Y   H   O
T   O   W   A   R   M
U   R   S   K   H   S
I   N   Y   R   D   S
```

WORD LIST

BUMPY **HOT** **SMOOTH** **COLD** **ROUGH** **SOFT**
DRY **SHARP** **WARM** **HARD** **SLIMY** **WET**

If you haven't found the answer, look carefully at all the unused letters in the word search.
They will spell out the missing words in this sentence:

What _____ _____ _____ _____ sense.

Test Your S.M.A.R.T.S.!

(SUPERIOR MENTAL ACUITY AND RATIONALITY TESTING SYSTEM)

AFTER MAKING IT ALL THE WAY THROUGH THIS CHAPTER, I SENSE THAT YOU'RE READY TO TAKE ON ANOTHER ONE OF MY HEAD-SPINNING QUIZZES.
(Get it? *Sense?* Ha!)

See if your brain has grown enough to get all four of these answers right. Don't forget that you can flip back through the chapter to find the information you need if your brain needs a boost! Also, just a reminder: There's a hidden word in each set of answers, if you're still up for it.

1. What is the sensory cortex?

Y The part of your brain that receives messages from your sense organs, like your eyes, ears, mouth, and nose

E The part of your brain that makes you sensitive

S The part of the brain that gives you common sense

E The part of the brain that makes you hungry and thirsty

Hidden Word: ___ ___ ___ ___

2. What is a supertaster?

T   Someone who can't taste anything

S   Someone who is a picky eater

E   Someone who is extra sensitive to tastes—especially bitter tastes

A   Someone who loves vegetables

Hidden Word: ____ ____ ____ ____

3. Some birds use Earth's magnetic field to help them _____.

I   migrate

R   fly

B   swim

D   take naps

Hidden Word: ____ ____ ____ ____

4. If you can taste numbers or smell musical notes, you might have _____.

E   the flu

O   chicken pox

T   prosopagnosia

N   synesthesia

Hidden Word: ____ ____ ____ ____

RECORD YOUR ANSWERS HERE

1	2	3	4

YOU ARE HERE

Bet you can outwit Atom

Slightly smarter than you were an hour ago

Not a total blockhead

MASTERMIND METER

CHAPTER FOUR

Speak Up!

Your brain interprets sounds in your temporal lobe. Can you find your way there?

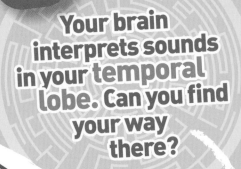

START HERE

Close your eyes ... No, not yet! You need to read my instructions first: Close your eyes and count how many different sounds you hear around you. When you're done counting, open your eyes and read on.

Unless you live in a hole underground, you could probably pick out about six sounds. Wait—you don't live in a hole, do you?

Assuming you live on Earth's surface, you can probably tell what's making those sounds, too: The gentle swish-swish is the dishwasher, the mumble is the TV in the other room, the crunching is your mom or dad pulling into the driveway.

Identifying sounds isn't as simple as it seems. In fact, the smartest scientists out there haven't been able to create a computer that identifies sounds as well as your brain does. Want to learn how your expert ears do their thing? Listen up!

How It Works

1

Ding dong!
The doorbell rings.
Vibrations from the sound
enter your ear. They beat
against your **eardrum**,
making it wiggle in
and out.

2

Next the sound
vibrations move into your
cochlea, a pool of liquid shaped
like a snail. The sound vibrations
create waves in the liquid. Your
cochlea is covered with millions of
tiny hairs. Eww—get the trimmer!
Just kidding. They're actually
hair cells.

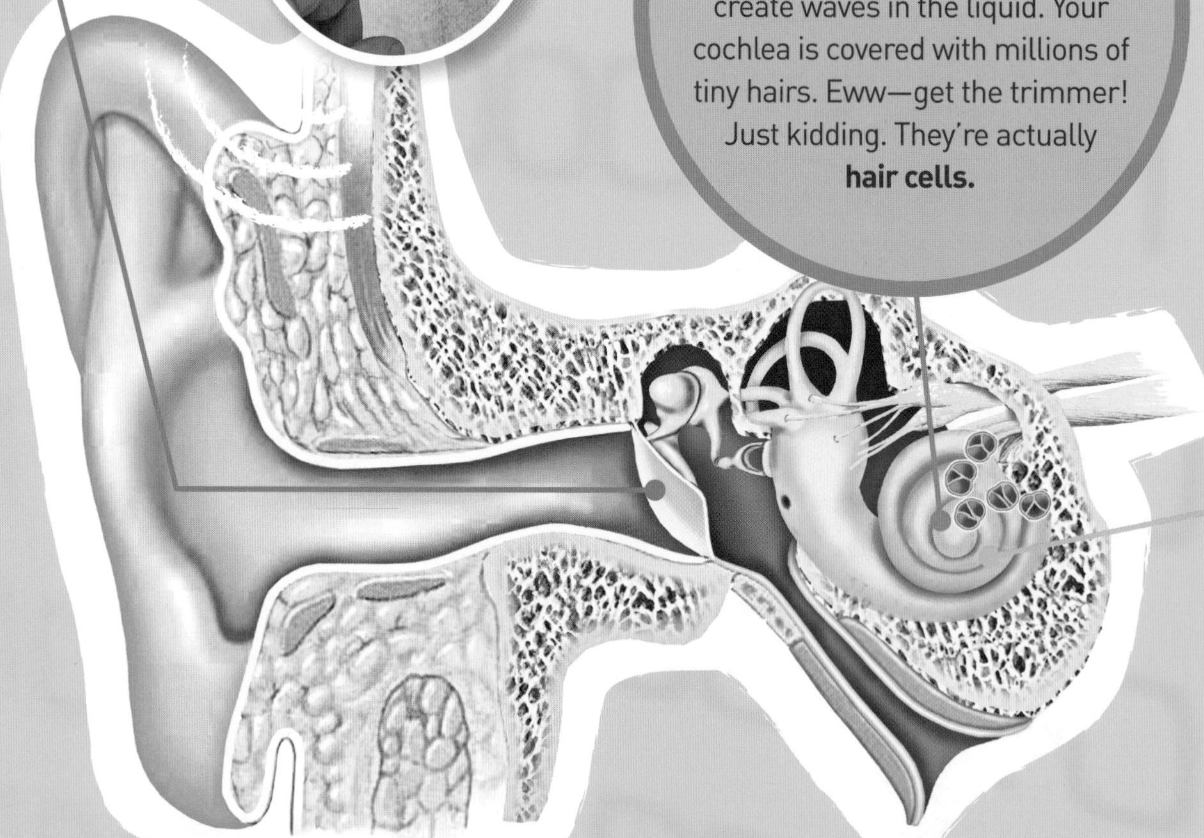

IMA GENIUS'S BRAINIAC BONUS: **NATURE MADE**

I am often found in shells, storms, and snails. If you connect the letters in the cor- rect order, using one continuous line that doesn't cross over itself, you will discover what I am. (Hint: Start at the red "A.")

S H A P
G S P I E C
N A L R A A
I D A L W
D E L
N I

3

Sound vibrations blow back your hair cells, bending them like tree branches on a windy day. The hair cells act like translators, turning the vibrations into electrical signals that the brain can understand. "Ding dong! Pizza's here!"

ATOM'S **BRAIN BREAK**

A tiger's skin is striped, just like its fur.

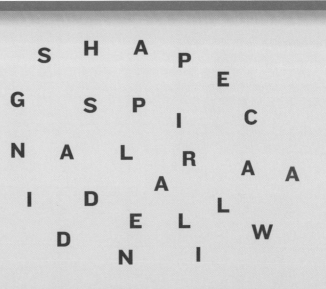

TiME TRiALS

So you feel like you're pretty fast at these already, huh? Ha! Your weak little noggin has a long way to go! Speed through these puzzles, and don't forget to record your time!

Solve this cryptogram to reveal a fact about your hearing. I bet it will surprise you! Use the cypher below to decode the secret message.

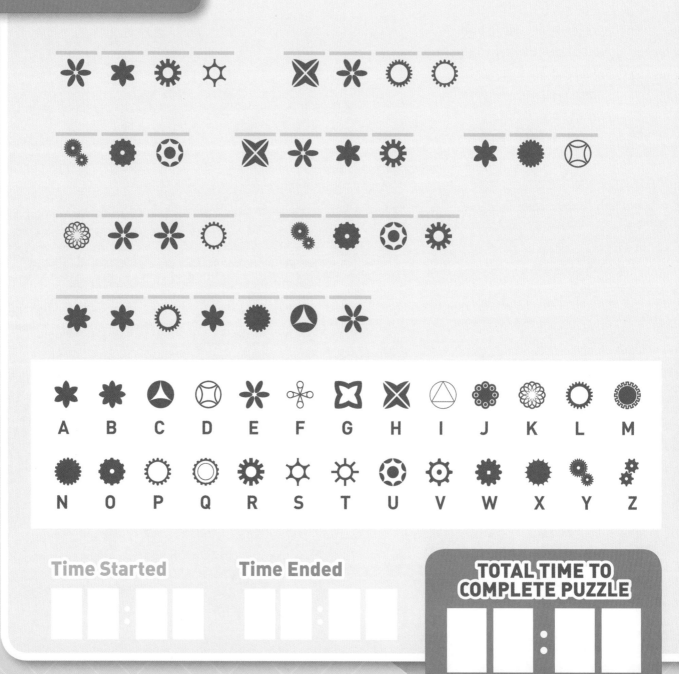

Time Started

Time Ended

TOTAL TIME TO COMPLETE PUZZLE

Follow the sound wave to the eardrum.
Enter the time you start and the time you finish.

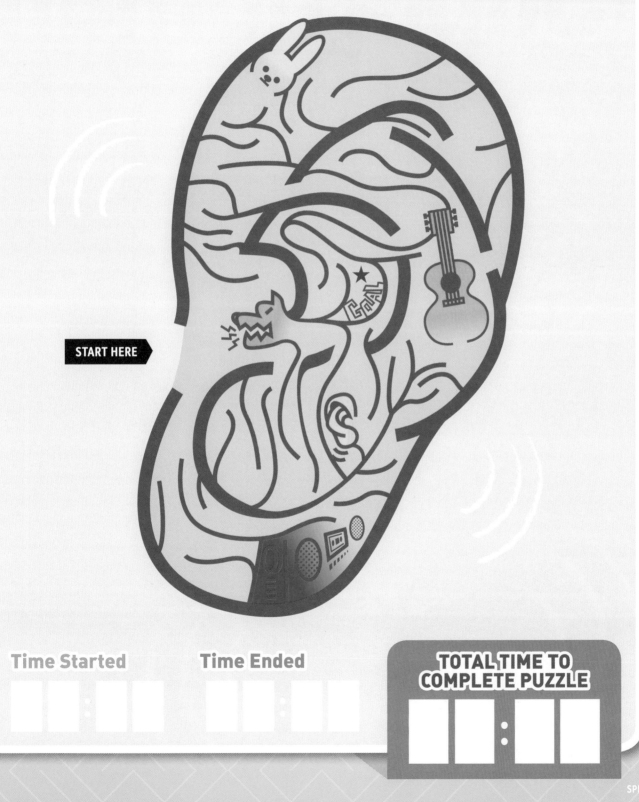

START HERE

Time Started

Time Ended

TOTAL TIME TO COMPLETE PUZZLE

Superhuman Hearing

YOU HUMANS HAVE PRETTY GOOD HEARING. Dogs, like me, have extraordinary ears. But these auditory aces put us both to shame!

NIGHT VISION

Ever heard the expression "blind as a bat"? It's not true. Bats can see, just not very well. But they don't need to: Their sense of hearing is so strong that they can "see" using their ears!

Bats use something called **echolocation** to fly in the dark. These night fliers emit high-pitched squeaks. The squeaks bounce off the ground, trees, and tasty bugs and head back to the bat's ears. They give the bat a 3-D map of its surroundings.

So don't challenge these hearing experts to a game of nighttime hide-and-seek—that's one game you're sure to lose!

X-RAY EARS

Like bats, dolphins use echolocation to "see" the world with their sense of hearing. Dolphins let out clicking sounds that bounce off nearby objects. By listening to the echoes, dolphins can sense where the objects are.

A dolphin's echolocation is so good that it can use it to find fish hiding beneath soft sand on the ocean floor. Dolphins can even tell the difference between clicks bouncing off a fish's soft skin and clicks bouncing off the fish's hard bones. That means the dolphins can actually detect a fish's skeleton: It's real live x-ray vision!

FINDERS KEEPERS

Ever wonder why you have two ears? You need a pair to help you figure out where sounds are coming from. If your dog is barking on your right, the sound reaches your right ear a tiny bit faster than it reaches your left ear. Your brain uses this difference to pinpoint where your dog is.

Owls do this best. Some owl species have crooked ear openings, with one ear higher and the other slightly more forward. This makes them superstars at finding where sounds are coming from. A tawny owl, for example, can pinpoint the exact position of a mouse in 0.01 seconds!

FUN FACT
The comic book superhero Daredevil hears just like a dolphin.

MASTER MOTH

So who's the gold medal animal champion of hearing? That title goes to this little guy: the greater wax moth. This moth has **ultrasonic** hearing—that means it can hear sounds that your human ears can't detect.

The highest pitched sound you can hear is about 20 kHz (think of the sound of screeching microphone feedback). Dogs like me can hear sounds at 45 kHz. Dog trainers use special high-pitched whistles at that pitch that we dogs can hear but you humans can't.

But the amazing greater wax moth can hear sounds at *300 kHz!* Scientists think they evolved this ability to help them outsmart their predators: bats, whose echolocating squeaks are super high-pitched. Now that's a spiffy sense to avoid becoming prey!

Flight Path

Bat Rhyme

Bats use their sonar to keep from crashing into one another, even when there are thousands flying in a group! Draw two separate circles of the same size, so that each bat is in at least one circle. Circles may touch or intersect.

GENIUS GENUS: SPATIAL SUPERSTAR

Unscramble the words below to complete the rhyme.

Though they are weak of _____,
(thigs)

Bats are _____ of the _____.
(streams)   (thing)

With their high-pitched _____,
(scickl)

Which _____ off objects,
(cubeon)

from beetles to _____,
(kcribs)

They send out an ultrasonic _____,
(sundo)

So delicious _____ can be _____.
(sicnest)   (dofun)

_____ having to avoid starvation,
(gameinI)

If you had to use human _____!
(cooltoechain)

Solve these puzzles about the most extraordinary ears in the animal kingdom. Get stuck? I thought you might. I'll help you out—flip back to the previous page for clues.

Daphne Dolphin loves to snack on sea trout, but there is a school of salmon swimming nearby. Sea trout and salmon are hard to tell apart! Daphne will have to use echolocation to get an x-ray look at the fish to find the two trout hiding in this school.

Can you find both trout?

Deaf Drummer

EVELYN GLENNIE TOURS THE WORLD, PERFORMING FOR PACKED AUDITORIUMS ON THE DRUMS, XYLOPHONE, AND OTHER PERCUSSION INSTRUMENTS. She is one of the world's most famous living musicians. She is also deaf.

Glennie began losing her hearing at age eight. But she didn't let her deafness stop her from her dream of becoming a professional musician.

Hearing is the ability to sense vibrations. Vibrations create waves of sound that move through the air. Most people use their ears to sense these sound waves. But not Glennie. She uses her body!

Glennie plays barefoot, which helps her sense the vibration from the instruments through her feet. Glennie says that she senses low notes in her legs and feet and higher pitches in her chest, arms, and face.

Scientists aren't sure how she does it. Glennie thinks that just like her, we all may hear with more than just our ears. We just don't know it!

Evelyn Glennie

Blindness Boost

Blindness can have a strange side effect—it sometimes amplifies musical ability!

Someone who has **perfect pitch** can identify any musical note just by hearing it. Play a note on a piano, and a person with perfect pitch will be able to tell you, "That's an F-sharp." Honk your car horn, and they'll be able to tell you what note that is, too! Perfect pitch is an extremely rare talent—only about one in 10,000 people have it.

But in the blind community, perfect pitch might be common. Scientists tested one group of blind children and found that about half had perfect pitch. These kids' brains may be using the portion normally devoted to vision for boosting their other senses.

MYTHS
BUSTED!

MYTH: Different parts of your tongue detect different tastes.

BUSTED!: Any part of your tongue can detect any taste. **BONUS:** Many people think there are just four tastes, but there are actually five! Besides sweet, salty, bitter, and sour, your tongue can detect a fifth one, umami, which means rich or savory.

By now, you've learned a little about how hearing works in your brain—now put it to the test! Challenge your brain with these puzzles and activities. They're easy for me, but then again ... pretty much everything is.

What Was That?

Your brain blocks out background noises so they don't distract you. But if you listen, you can hear them. Turn off any distracting sounds like music or the TV. Now the room seems quiet, but it really isn't! Listen in and see how many noises you can name. (Answers could be things like road noise outside, birds, the dishwasher, your heart beating.)

_____   _____

_____   _____

_____   _____

Flip Out

GENIUS GENUS: WORD WIZARD

To find the reason bats don't need good eyesight, flip five letters above or below the line. Do not move any letters to the right or left.

U   THR   SORNI
_____
  L   EAA   INCG

Noisy World

GENIUS GENUS: LOGICAL LEADER

The items below make noises that are very quiet or very loud. The volume of these noises is measured in decibels. Exposure to 85 decibels for eight hours can cause permanent damage to your ears. Sounds at 120 decibels can cause immediate damage! Can you match the objects to their decibel levels?

| 30 | 45 | 70 | 85–90 | 88 | 98 | 110 | 110 | 130–150 | 140 |

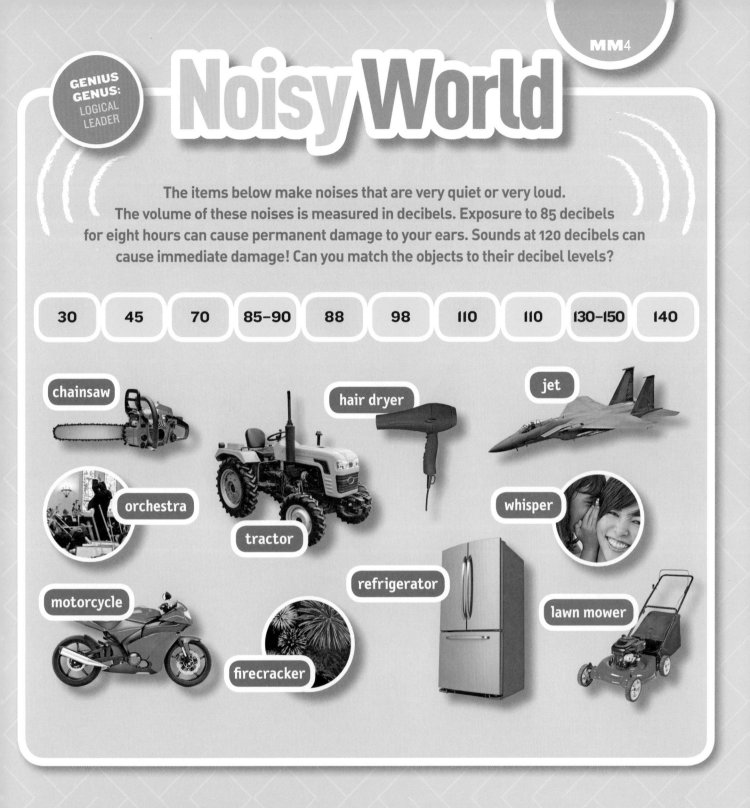

chainsaw

orchestra

tractor

hair dryer

jet

whisper

motorcycle

firecracker

refrigerator

lawn mower

Riddle

Even the smallest horseback rider can't fit his or her foot into this stirrup. It's made of bone, not leather, and rests between an anvil and a hammer. Where will you find this stirrup?

Ear to Ear

Ears can be deceptive. Large ears don't always belong to large animals, and small ears don't always belong to small animals. Can you name the animal that each set of ears belongs to? The box below has all the answers ... but they are scrambled and not in order!

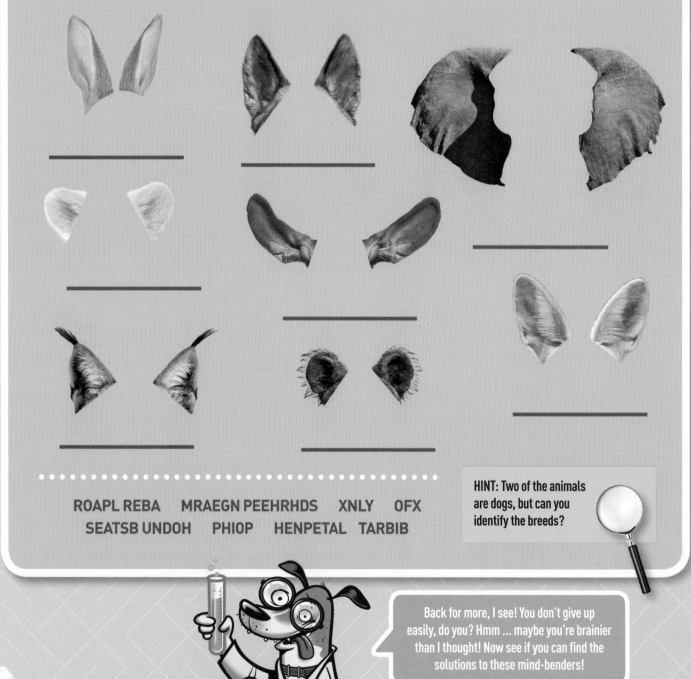

ROAPL REBA   MRAEGN PEEHRHDS   XNLY   OFX

SEATSB UNDOH   PHIOP   HENPETAL   TARBIB

HINT: Two of the animals are dogs, but can you identify the breeds?

Back for more, I see! You don't give up easily, do you? Hmm ... maybe you're brainier than I thought! Now see if you can find the solutions to these mind-benders!

Missing Letters

Sometimes we miss what other people are saying because our brain is focusing on something else. That's what happened here. This person tried to write down what someone else was saying, but he only caught part of the sentence. (Fortunately, we found the missing letters.)

Can you complete the sentence?

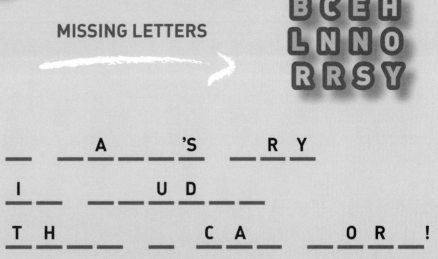

MISSING LETTERS

A A A B
B C E H
L N N O
R R S Y

___ ___ A ___ ___ ___ 'S ___ R Y

I ___ ___ ___ ___ U D ___ ___ ___

T H ___ ___ ___ ___ C A ___ ___ O R ___ !

Out of Order

Someone moved these columns out of order. Fortunately, each word in the message is a unique color. Can you reorder the columns to reveal an interesting fact?

E		S	C	S	C	K	I	T	R	E	U
	G		I	E	T	R	E	L	H		S
	N	E	T	E		O		S			S
	V	S	N	A	S	D	U	W	O		E

HINT: Copy or trace the grid on a separate piece of paper and cut out the columns to match them up.

Test Your S.M.A.R.T.S.!

(SUPERIOR MENTAL ACUITY AND RATIONALITY TESTING SYSTEM)

WOW, I MUST ADMIT THAT YOU CONQUERED MY HEARING PUZZLES FASTER THAN I EXPECTED.

But you have one more task ahead of you before you can move on to the next chapter.

It's time to test how much you know about your sense of sound. Answer these questions with information from the chapter you just read ... if your teensy thinker can handle it! (Don't forget to hunt for the word hidden in each set of answers!)

1. _____ turn sounds into the electrical signals your brain can understand.

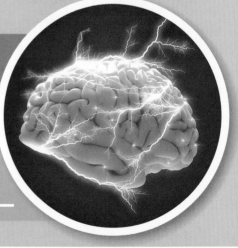

N Nerves

R Eardrums

U Hair cells

T Electricians

Hidden Word: ___ ___ ___ ___

2. _____ and _____ are two animals in this chapter that use echolocation to sense the world around them.

H   Humans, elephants

E   Dogs, cats

O   Bats, dolphins

C   Squid, octopuses

Hidden Word: ____ ____ ____ ____

3. What does the greater wax moth's super sense of hearing help it do?

M   Stay away from its predator: bats

T   Fly faster

H   Navigate through the forest

O   Enjoy the opera

Hidden Word: ____ ____ ____ ____ ____

4. Someone who can identify a musical note just by hearing it has _____.

A   prosopagnosia   R   perfect pitch

E   synesthesia   H   star power

Hidden Word: ____ ____ ____ ____

RECORD YOUR ANSWERS HERE

1 2 3 4

You're pretty intelligent ... for a primate

YOU ARE HERE

Bet you can outwit Atom

Slightly smarter than you were an hour ago

Not a total blockhead

MASTERMIND METER

CHAPTER FIVE

Run Fast, Jump High

Walk your way to the top of the motor cortex.

START HERE

Well done, budding egghead! You've made it halfway through the book. You are no longer the mental weakling you were in chapter 1, but we still have a long way to go. So read along and picture this:

It's recess, and you're playing basketball. Your teammate catches your eye and tosses the ball in your direction. As it arcs through the sky, your body angles toward where it's heading. Your sneakers come down in the perfect spot; your hands stretch out. The ball falls into your waiting palms. You turn, you leap, you throw, and ... swoosh! Perfect shot.

To make your sweet two-pointer, your brain had to send complex, lightning-fast signals to tiny muscles all over your body. I bet you never even realized this was going on, did you? Well, time to think about ... how you think about your body!

How It Works

1

Your **motor cortex** is the boss of your movement system. It controls movement in every part of your body, from arching your eyebrows to wiggling your toes. It sets plans and goals but leaves the details to the other parts of the body. Bottom line: The motor cortex gives the orders, and your body does its bidding. That's my kind of brain part!

2

The brain sends a signal to the **spinal cord.** Like in a relay race, the spinal cord passes the signal on all the way to your toes.

Your muscles and joints have **sensors** that keep track of where all your body parts are. As you balance, the sensors in your toes send signals back to the brain. The brain responds with directions to correct your position by moving tiny muscles.

Motor cortex says:
"OK, body, it looks like we're on a balance beam. Muscles and joints, you balance us."

Spinal cord says:
"Ready, set, go!"

Muscles and joints say:
"A little to the left! Whoa, too far—now lean right!"

ATOM'S **BRAIN BREAK**

Just like fingerprints, everyone's tongue print is different.

Use your motor cortex to write down the message below.
Use the cypher to decode the secret message.

You know what to do. It's time to see if your slowpoke brain is getting any speedier. Grab a pencil and go, go, go!

A	B	C	D	E	F	G	H	I	J	K	L	M

N	O	P	Q	R	S	T	U	V	W	X	Y	Z

Time Started

Time Ended

TOTAL TIME TO COMPLETE PUZZLE

Follow the signals down to the red star at the bottom of the spinal cord. Remember to enter the time you start and finish.

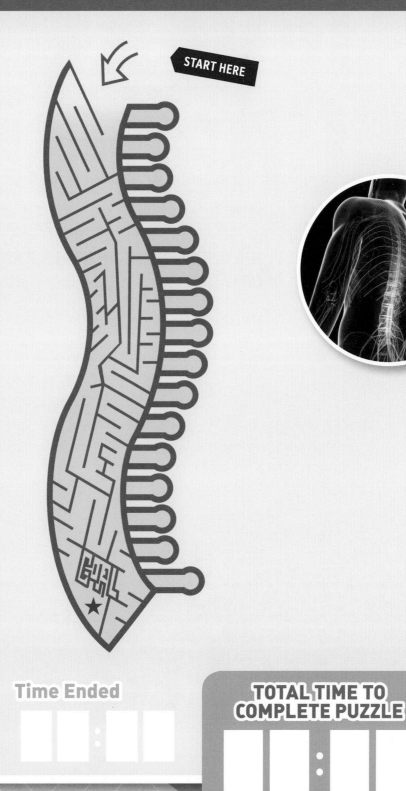

START HERE

GOAL

Time Started

Time Ended

TOTAL TIME TO
COMPLETE PUZZLE

Animal Champions

IT'S A GOOD THING ANIMALS CAN'T ENTER THE OLYMPICS! These gold medal winners of the wild would leave you humans in the dust. How do they get their champion moves? From their brains, of course!

FASTER THAN A FERRARI

A cheetah can go from 0 to 60 miles an hour (97 km/h) in only three seconds—that's faster than most sports cars! The cheetah hides in tall grass on the African savanna. It sneaks within about 50 feet (15 m) of its prey, then—zoom!—it takes off.

Even at top speeds of 70 miles an hour (113 km/h), the cheetah performs nimble twists and turns to outmaneuver its prey. When the cheetah wants to change direction, it whips its tail the opposite way. Like a rudder on a boat, this helps the cheetah steer. That antelope never had a chance!

TINY BUT MIGHTY

The highest jumper in the animal kingdom is so tiny you can barely see it! This teensy insect, called the spittlebug, is only 0.2 inches (0.5 cm) long—but it can leap 28 inches (71 cm) into the air. That's the equivalent of you jumping over a seven-story building! The spittlebug's secret? Two supercharged muscles in its chest power its legs. As the spittlebug gets ready to jump, it tucks up its hind legs then snaps them straight. The bug goes flying!

HEAVY LIFTER

Benedikt Magnusson, an Icelandic strong-man, set a deadlift world record by lifting 1,015 pounds (460 kg). That's 2.7 times his body weight! But Magnusson is a weakling compared to the lifting cham-pion of the animal kingdom: the Hercu-les beetle. This 0.7-ounce (20 g) insect can lift 850 times its own weight—the equivalent of a human hoisting more than a dozen cars with each arm!

SAILING TO VICTORY

Olympians like Michael Phelps can blaze through water at nearly six miles an hour (10 km/h). But compared to the speedy sailfish, that's nothing! Sailfish cruise at 68 miles an hour (109 km/h)—about as fast as a car goes on the highway! This makes them the fastest swim-mers on Earth. They get their speed from powerful fins, which keep them sailing out of reach of hungry sharks.

FUN FACT

Motion sickness happens when your body's balance centers get confused.

Jumpers

To find the answer to the question below, use the clues on the left to unscramble the words. Then unscramble the letters in the yellow boxes.

Kids play me to test their jumping skills. What am I?

CLUES	SCRAMBLED WORDS	ANSWER
I might jump three feet (0.9m) high and flick my feet when I'm happy.	BIBART	_ _ _ _ _ _
There's a whole sport built around jumping, just for me.	SHORE	_ _ _ _ _
I can jump 7 inches (18 cm) high and 13 inches (33 cm) in distance off a dog.	LEAF	_ _ _ _
With a running start, I can jump almost 30 feet (9 m).	IAMLAP	_ _ _ _ _ _
Scientists aren't quite sure why I jump out of the water, but I know how to put on a show!	PINHOLD	_ _ _ _ _ _ _
I'm colorful, roughly three inches (7.6 cm) long, and spend most of my life high above the ground.	RETE ORGF	_ _ _ _ _ _ _ _
My back legs are like miniature but powerful catapults, shooting me into the air as far as 20 inches (51 cm).	RAGSPERSHOP	_ _ _ _ _ _ _ _ _ _ _
I'm actually a group of arachnids, some of which can spring up to 50 times their body length.	GUMJINP REDSIP	_ _ _ _ _ _ _ _ _ _ _ _ _

ANSWER ⬜⬜⬜⬜⬜⬜⬜⬜

I start jumping whenever I see a ball ... errr ... I mean ... well done, student.

Herculean Task

Four Hercules beetles have stumbled across a two-pound (0.9-kg) table filled with 22 pounds (about 10 kg) of delicious food that would feed their entire family. The only problem is choosing which items to carry home. Hercules beetles are extremely strong for their size. They can each carry up to 37 pounds (about 17 kg), but since they are only a few inches (cm) long, they can only carry one item at a time. Which of the items should the beetles take to get the most food back home?

BUCKET FULL OF DECAYING LEAVES
4 POUNDS (1.8 kg)

TREE SAPLING
3 POUNDS (1.4 kg)

ROTTING WOOD
5 POUNDS (2.3 kg)

CAKE
5 POUNDS (2.3 kg)

TURKEY
2 POUNDS (0.9 kg)

APPLES
3 POUNDS (1.4 kg)

Mind Machines

IN 2008, A MONKEY MOVED A ROBOTIC ARM ... USING ONLY ITS MIND. Sitting still in a chair, the monkey made the robot arm grab grapes and marshmallows and push the snacks into its mouth.

How is this possible? Scientists implanted a tiny device in the monkey's brain. They placed it on the part of the motor cortex that controls arm and hand movements. Wires connected the brain implant to a robotic arm. When the monkey's brain tried to send signals to the monkey's arm, telling it to move, the signals went to the robot arm instead.

Within days, the monkey learned to use the robotic arm to grab snacks placed in front of it. At first, the monkey was clumsy, missing its mouth. But as it practiced, its brain adapted and it got better at the task. Soon the monkey was using the robot arm to feed itself as fast as food was put in front of it. That's no monkey business!

MYTHS BUSTED!

MYTH: Fingers wrinkle in the tub because they absorb water.

BUSTED!: Your nerve endings actually tell your brain to deflate your fingers when they get soaked. Experiments show that wrinkly fingers make it easier to grip wet objects, the same way tire treads help cars cling to rainy roads.

Robo Man

Twenty-nine-year-old Julian Pinto is paralyzed from the waist down. But at the 2014 World Cup in Brazil, he walked onto the field and kicked off the ball to officially begin the games. How did he do it?

Pinto wore a robotic suit that he controlled using his brain. Just like the monkey with the robot arm, Pinto retrained his brain to move the suit instead of moving his body. Scientists hope this technology will help all kinds of paralyzed people walk, run, kick, and dance again. Now that's some spiffy science!

IMA GENIUS'S BRAINIAC BONUS: **DOG-GONE SMART**

A group of dogs wearing doggie backpacks are on their way to bring supplies to some injured people at a campsite. First the dogs must cross a stream in a canoe. They only have one chance to cross the stream before the water makes it too dangerous. The middle of the canoe must stay empty. Decide how to arrange this group so the front and back of the canoe are perfectly balanced. If you'd like, you can remove the dogs' backpacks. Weights are written on each dog and its backpack.

3

Max
25

2

Gazer
6

Mitsi
4

3

1

5

Kei-Ko
18

Jack
13

Your brain controls your body so precisely that you can do everything from balance on a bike to grab a Frisbee out of midair. But sometimes, your body plays tricks on your brain! Try out these movement experiments to see what I mean.

Spinning Test

Stand up straight with your arms out. Spin around as fast as you can four times, then stop. What sensation do you notice?

When you stop spinning, you'll feel like you're still moving—a sensation we call dizziness. Why does it happen? That's your **vestibular sense,** your sense of balance, in action. Inside each ear, you have tiny tubs of liquid. When you spin, the liquid spins too, pressing down the tiny hair cells in your inner ear. When you stop spinning suddenly, the liquid keeps going—your brain thinks your body is still moving! This makes you dizzy.

Want to spin around without getting dizzy? Use this trick: After you spin one direction, spin the opposite direction. This will cancel out the motion of the liquid in your inner ear.

Pinocchio Nose

Try this illusion to see what it would feel like to have a nose as long as Pinocchio's!

STEP 1: Blindfold yourself and stand behind a friend.

STEP 2: Reach one hand around and stroke, tap, and rub your friend's nose. At the same time, exactly copy the movements with your other hand on your own nose. Make the sequence of movements as random as possible. Continue for 60 seconds.

WHOA, WHAT HAPPENED? After about 30 to 40 seconds, your nose will seem to move to someplace else. Some people feel like their nose grows as long as Pinocchio's! The body sends signals to the brain. The brain tries to make sense of them, but sometimes, it gets it wrong!

Confuse Your Legs

Your body always does what you tell it, right? Maybe not...

STEP 1: While sitting down, lift your right foot a few inches (cm) from the floor. Circle your leg continuously in a clockwise direction.

STEP 2: Now draw a number 6 in the air using your right index finger.

WHOA, WHAT HAPPENED? Your foot starts turning in a counterclockwise direction, even if you try to stop it! That's because the left side of your brain, which controls the right side of your body, deals with rhythm. It won't let you make two opposite movements at the same time.

Twisted Hands

1. Holding your hands out in front of you, rotate your wrists inward so the tops of your hands are facing each other.
2. Cross your right hand over your left and clasp your fingers together.
3. Bending your elbows, bring your hands down and toward your body and twist your arms up until your hands are right under your chin. Make sure to hold your hands out from your chest—don't let them touch your body.
4. Have a friend or parent point to one of your fingers without touching it. Try to wiggle it.
5. Try it with different fingers. Weird, huh?

The Twisted Hands test messes with your **proprioception,** or your sense of where your body is in space. Proprioception is the reason you always know where your arms and legs are, even when your eyes are closed. The Twisted Hands test tricks that sense, fooling your brain into thinking that your hands have switched position.

It's All Related

GENIUS
GENUS:
WORD
WIZARD

Enter the groups of letters below to the right or left of the center column (in yellow) to form words from this chapter. Then fill in the column by guessing the missing letter for each word. The words you build will give you a clue about the word in the center column. If you need help, see the hint below.

I bet your brain is feeling a little foolish after those tricky tests on the last page. Time to show off what your noggin knows!

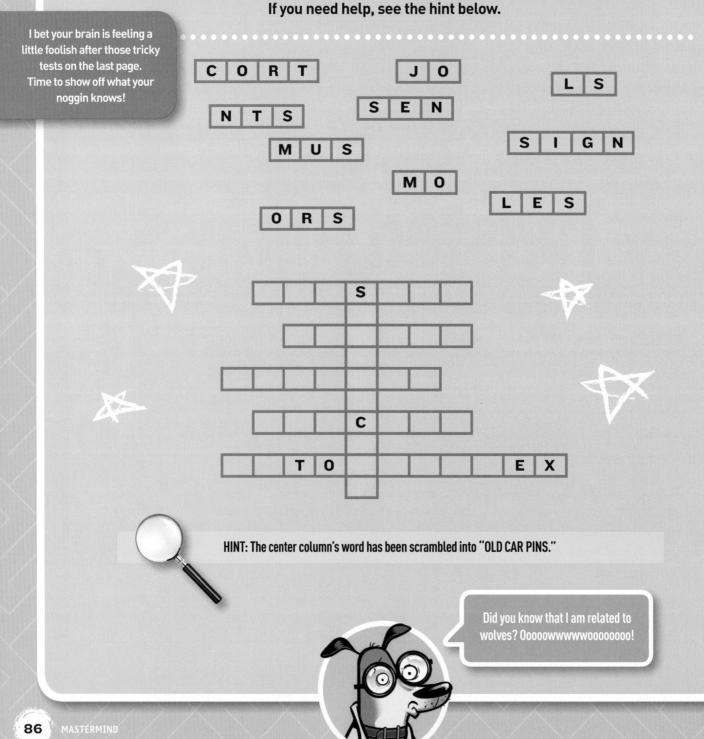

| C | O | R | T |

| J | O |

| L | S |

| N | T | S |

| S | E | N |

| S | I | G | N |

| M | U | S |

| M | O |

| L | E | S |

| O | R | S |

S

C

T O

E X

HINT: The center column's word has been scrambled into "OLD CAR PINS."

Did you know that I am related to wolves? Oooooowwwwwwooooooooo!

Letter Swap

Two letters have been swapped throughout the entire puzzle below.
Unswap the letters to reveal the hidden message.

W	E	D	O	T	N	J	U	S	N	G	E	N	S
E	T	S	A	N	I	O	T	S	F	R	O	M	O
U	R	A	R	M	S	A	T	D	L	E	G	S	.
O	U	R	I	T	N	E	R	T	A	L	O	R	G
A	T	S	C	A	T	S	E	T	D	N	H	E	M
N	O	O	.	H	U	T	G	E	R	P	A	I	T
S	L	E	N	Y	O	U	K	T	O	W	I	N	I
S	N	I	M	E	N	O	E	A	N	!			

Hidden Truth

When you are scared or cold, tiny muscles make the hairs on your skin stand upright,
causing this common occurrence. In our hairier ancestors, this made them look larger to frighten
off what was scaring them. It also trapped warm air beneath their body hair, warming them up.

Can you follow the instructions below to reveal this natural event?

1. Cross out all the vowels in columns 1, 4, 9, 10.
2. Find the first and last letters of the grid.
   Cross out these letters everywhere.
3. Change all Ts to Ms.
4. Cross out all letters found in "HAIR".
5. Change all Zs to Os.
6. Cross out the 3rd letter of columns 2, 5, 7, 8.
7. Cross out everywhere "DM" appear together, in this order.
8. Cross out the 1st letter of columns 2, 4, 8.
9. There will be one letter left in each column. Write it in the space below to spell the answer!

1	2	3	4	5	6	7	8	9	10
C	S	C	N	E	H	H	S	P	K
G	I	Z	D	M	R	K	I	K	I
R	Z	C	H	M	B	G	B	O	S
E	Z	R	E	H	A	K	T	D	T
I	R	I	S	D	T	U	D	M	K

Test Your S.M.A.R.T.S.!

(SUPERIOR MENTAL ACUITY AND RATIONALITY TESTING SYSTEM)

NOT BAD, STUDENT! WHY, I CAN PRACTICALLY SEE YOUR BRAIN BULGING AS YOU READ. In fact, is that a little bit of your motor cortex coming out of your ear? Ha! Made you look.

Your brain is no match for mine just yet. But why don't you try to prove me wrong? Give this quiz your best shot! Then solve the bonus challenge by finding all four hidden words.

1. Your motor cortex controls _____,

I smiling

B dancing

S driving a car

D all of the above

Hidden Word: ___ ___ ___ ___ ___

2. What animal can go from 0 to 60 miles an hour (97 km/h) faster than most sports cars?

A Racehorse
T Gazelle
F Cheetah
S *T. rex*

Hidden Word: ____ ____ ____ ____

3. In 2008, a monkey moved _____ just by thinking.

O a forklift
M a toy train
V a robotic arm
E another monkey

Hidden Word: ____ ____ ____ ____ ____

4. Your vestibular sense is your sense of _____.

F balance
L smell
E taste
E humor

Hidden Word: ____ ____ ____ ____

RECORD YOUR ANSWERS HERE

1	2	3	4

Budding egghead

YOU ARE HERE

You're pretty intelligent ... for a primate

Bet you can outwit Atom

Slightly smarter than you were an hour ago

Not a total blockhead

MASTERMIND METER

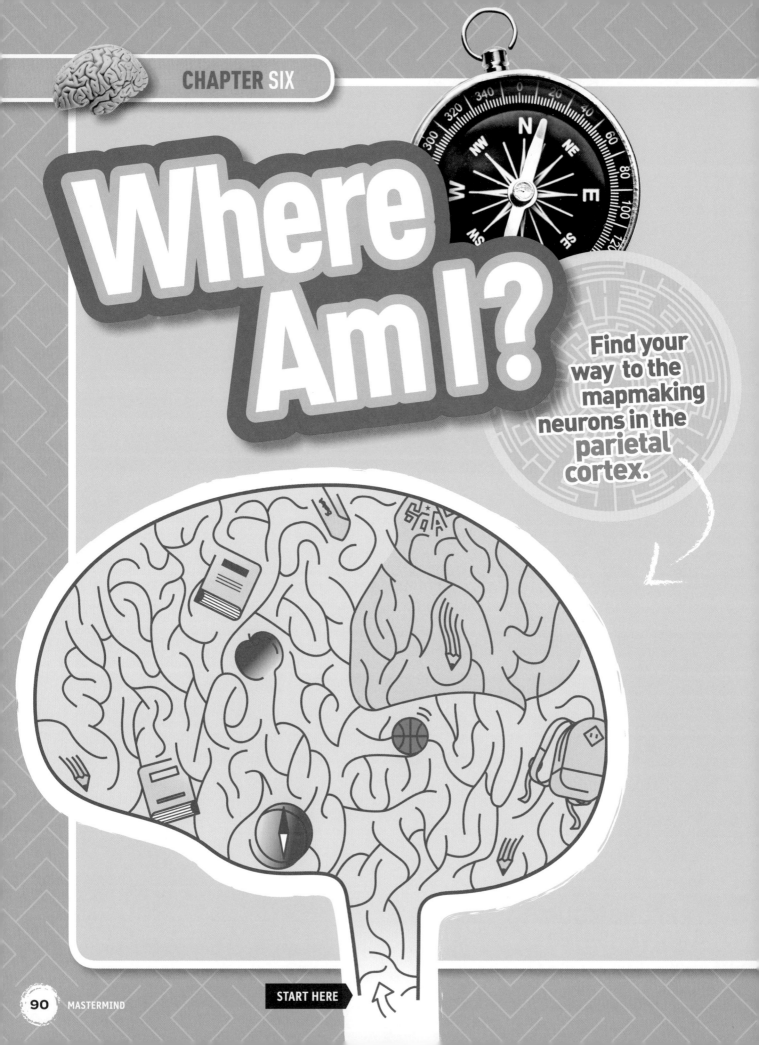

CHAPTER SIX

Where Am I?

Find your way to the mapmaking neurons in the parietal cortex.

START HERE

Good news, genius-in-training! After that last chapter, it looks like your once-empty noggin is really filling up with incredible information! Kudos to you for working so hard to beef up your brain.

Building brainpower isn't always so much work. Did you know that sometimes your brain learns by itself, without you even trying? Consider this:

When you first start at a new school, the whole place is unfamiliar. You don't know where the bathrooms are or which way to the gym. But fast-forward just a few days, and you can find your way around with your eyes closed. It's almost like you've memorized a map ... but you never studied. The human brain is incredibly talented at making mental maps. How does it do it? Turn the page to find out!

How It Works

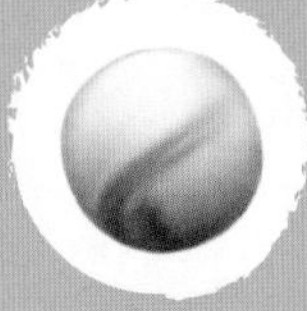

2

Neurons in your **parietal cortex** calculate the direction and speed of the ball, creating a split-second mental map of its path across the field. At the same time, these neurons also calculate the direction you should run to intercept the ball. You take off toward the spot.

1

You're in the out-field when—*thwack!*—the batter smacks the ball, sending it skimming over the ground.

4 You pop upright. Neurons in your **hippocampus** check your mental map to figure out which way to turn your body to aim at second base. Your arm whips the ball. It smacks into the glove. The runner's out! The crowd goes wild!

3 As you get close, other neurons adjust the position of your body to put you in the right spot to grab the ball. You dive, your arm outstretched. *Thunk!*—the ball skips into your glove.

IMA GENIUS'S BRAINIAC BONUS: **CALCULATING**

No one knows what this sequence of numbers means. Can you determine the message?

HINT: You may want to use a calculator to help you, but it's not necessary.

53045 733 57735 302

TIME TRIALS

Discover an awesome fact about your parietal cortex and hippocampus. Use the cypher below to decode the secret message.

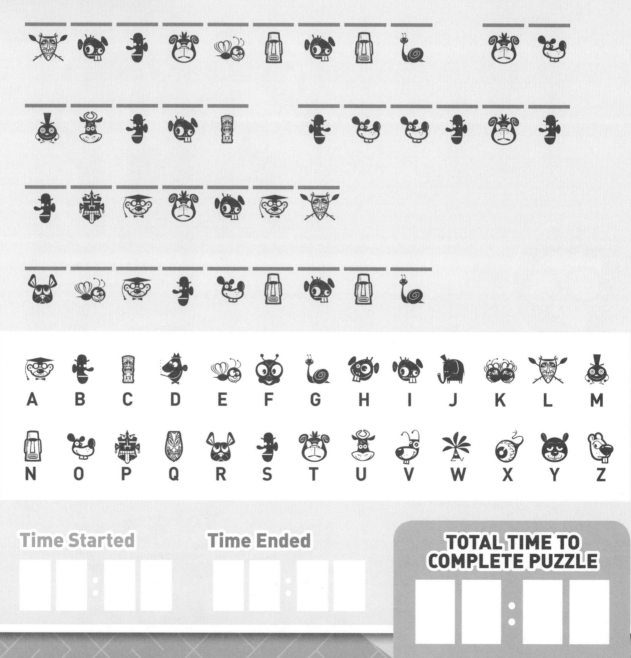

Time Started

Time Ended

TOTAL TIME TO COMPLETE PUZZLE

Find your way through the neuron to its nucleus—the cell's control center. Remember to enter the time you start and finish.

GOAL

START HERE

Time Started

Time Ended

TOTAL TIME TO COMPLETE PUZZLE

Taxi Brain

VISIT LONDON, ENGLAND, AND YOU MIGHT NOTICE PEOPLE SPEEDING AROUND THE CITY ON SCOOTERS, STUDYING CLIPBOARDS ATTACHED TO THEIR HANDLEBARS.

These men and women are taxi drivers–in–training. To pass the test to get a license, they have to learn "the Knowledge," a memorized map of the city. It's no easy feat—with its 25,000 streets and thousands of landmarks, London is like a maze!

London taxi drivers don't use maps or a GPS, so all these details have to be stored in their brains. Learning the Knowledge well enough to pass the test takes most people at least four years. Some call it the toughest test in the world!

In 1999, a group of scientists looked at images of London taxi drivers' brains. What they found surprised them. The brains of drivers who had passed the test looked different from average brains. The **hippocampus,** the area that stores mental maps, was bigger.

This study showed scientists that learning can actually change the shape of your brain! Like a muscle, the brain really does get bigger the more you use it.

MYTHS
BUSTED!

MYTH: This is a photo of London Bridge.

BUSTED!: This is London Bridge! Not much to look at, huh?

ATOM'S **BRAIN BREAK**

An ostrich's brain is smaller than its eye. What a birdbrain!

Driving You Nuts

Ready to work out your noggin? Get to it!

Just like taxi drivers use their spatial memory to find London landmarks, squirrels use theirs to find food they've hidden.

Sam the squirrel needs to bury six nuts. His nut-burying steps are listed below. Use the grid to mark where Sam buries each nut (1 through 6).

After Sam moves, he faces the new direction.

1. Sam is standing on the spot labeled "start."
2. Sam faces north, then hops two squares to his right.
3. Sam faces east and hops three squares to his left.
4. Sam faces north and hops one square to his left and buries a nut on that spot.
5. Sam repeats steps 2 through 4 to bury two more nuts.
6. After Sam buries Nut #3, he turns south and hops forward four squares.
7. Sam hops two squares to his right and buries another nut.
8. Sam repeats his original pattern to bury Nuts #5 and 6.

Remember where you bury the nuts. That will keep you from getting lost!

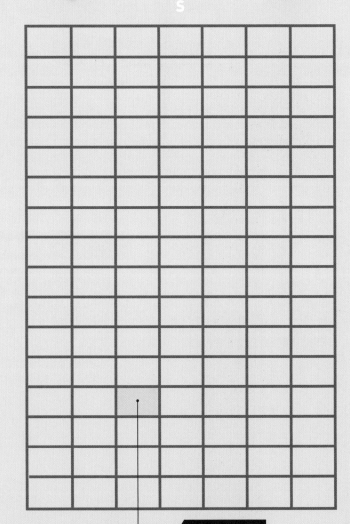

START HERE

This is nuts!

Cube Confusion

If you were to fold the picture below into a cube, which cube (A, B, C, or D) would it match?

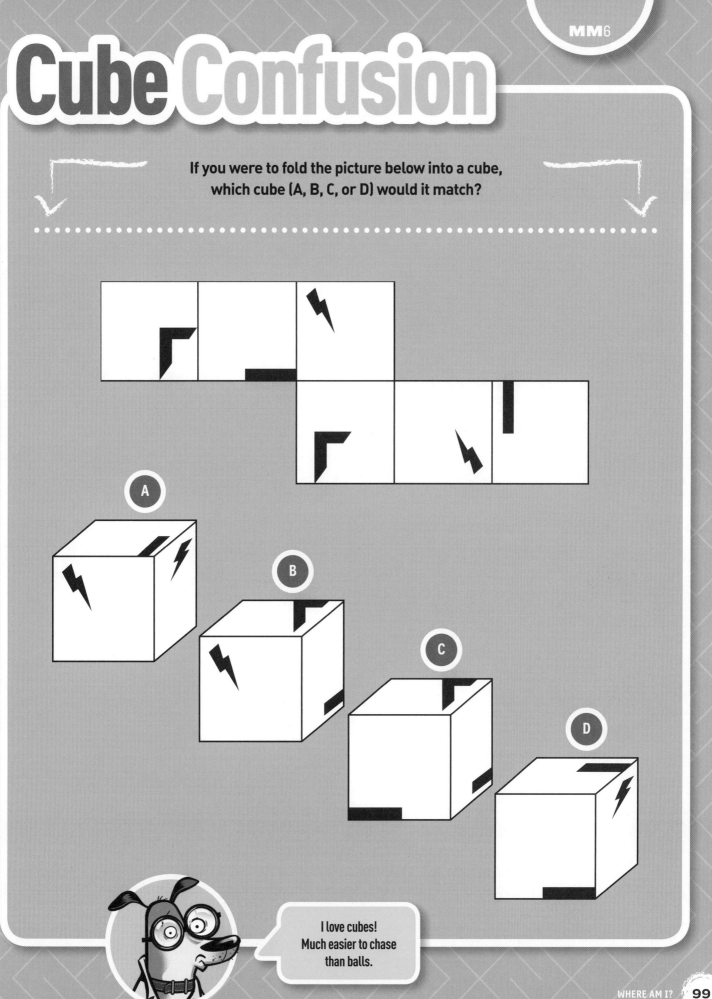

I love cubes!
Much easier to chase
than balls.

The Man Who Ignores Half the World

IF YOU GIVE ALAN BURGESS A PICTURE OF A PIG AND ASK HIM TO COPY IT, YOU'LL SEE A STRANGE SKETCH. HIS DRAWING ONLY SHOWS THE RIGHT HALF OF THE ANIMAL!

Alan has a condition called **hemispatial neglect:** His brain ignores everything on his left side. People with Alan's condition may shave only one side of their face, or eat the food from only one half of their plate. For them, one half of the world simply doesn't exist.

Here's the strangest thing: There's nothing wrong with Alan's eyes. People with hemispatial neglect can see things on both sides perfectly fine. Ask Alan to copy a picture of a house, and his drawing will be missing the fence on the left side of the page. But if you point out the fence and ask him what it is, he'll say, "A fence, of course!"

If you ask him why he didn't draw it, he might say, "It will probably blow down as soon as there's a wind, so I didn't bother." He's not lying on purpose—since his eyes can see the fence, his brain has to invent a reason that he didn't draw it. How tricky!

Whisker Power

Getting around is tough for someone like Alan Burgess, whose eyes and brain don't communicate correctly. We humans rely on our vision to help us navigate. So how do creatures that prowl around in the dark, like cats, find their way?

Your cat's secret night-vision tool? Her whiskers! Whiskers are so sensitive they can sense the slightest change in air currents. When Fluffy is slinking around the living room at night, tiny air currents are bouncing off the couches and chairs. Her whiskers tell her where these obstacles are and keep her from crashing into them, even in complete darkness.

Fragile Package

GENIUS GENUS:
SPATIAL SUPERSTAR

Amanda left a few items at home when she left for college: a pair of boots, a book, and a glass water goblet, which is fragile. If you pack everything so all the items fit snugly in the correct box, the goblet won't break. How would you arrange the items, and which box would be a perfect fit? Hint: You can flip and turn the items in any direction needed for packing.

BOX A

BOX B

Chemistry for Kids

There are two types of spatial intelligence. Most people have one or the other, but not both. To find out which type of spatial genius you have, try both of these puzzles.

Run Around

As a delivery person, you need to know the fastest way through this busy city. Every turn you make at a corner will slow you down. Draw the quickest, most efficient route to complete all your deliveries. The destinations on the list are in no particular order. Start at the Red X. Count the number of turns it takes for you to deliver all your packages.

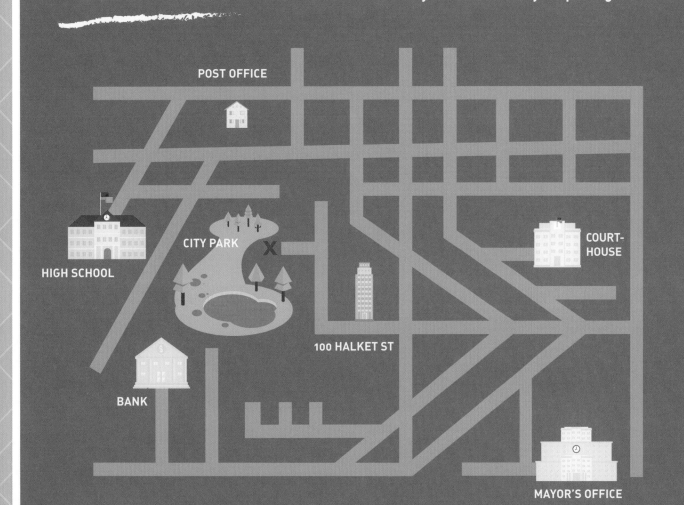

POST OFFICE

HIGH SCHOOL

CITY PARK

X

COURT-HOUSE

100 HALKET ST

BANK

MAYOR'S OFFICE

DESTINATIONS FOR PACKAGES:

- Post office
- Courthouse
- Mayor's office
- 100 Halket St.
- Bank
- High school

If Fragile Package was easier for you, you're a "Trunk Packer." Trunk Packers are good at mentally rearranging shapes. You use this skill when figuring out the best way to arrange luggage to fit in the trunk of a car. You also use it to imagine how something might look, such as a new set of furniture in your living room.

Einstein was famously good at this skill—he used his Trunk Packing genius to visualize how stars and planets pull on each other in space!

If Run Around was easier for you, you're a "Navigator." Navigators are good at looking at a two-dimensional map and relating it to the real, three-dimensional world.

Famous explorers like Magellan, the first person to plan a successful expedition all the way around the globe, were probably Navigators.

It's time to put your spatial skills to the test! If you're a Navigator, you might find you're super skilled at puzzles that test your ability to find your way, like Crazy Maze. If you're a Trunk Packer, you might breeze through puzzles that involve mentally manipulating objects, like Intersections.

GENIUS GENUS: SPATIAL SUPERSTAR

Intersections

The black image matches one of the red images. It is not a mirror image, but has been rotated. Which image does it match?

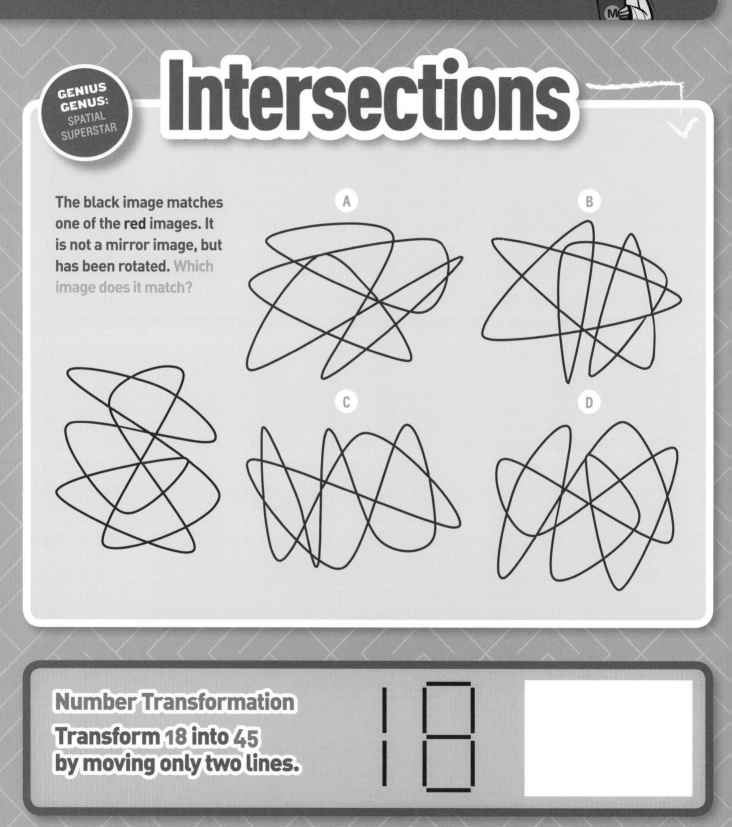

A   B

C   D

Number Transformation

Transform 18 into 45 by moving only two lines.

Crazy Maze

GENIUS GENUS: SPATIAL SUPERSTAR

Which of the maze pieces below (A, B, or C) is the correct match for this left puzzle piece?

Only one puzzle piece allows you to go from start to finish without getting stuck.

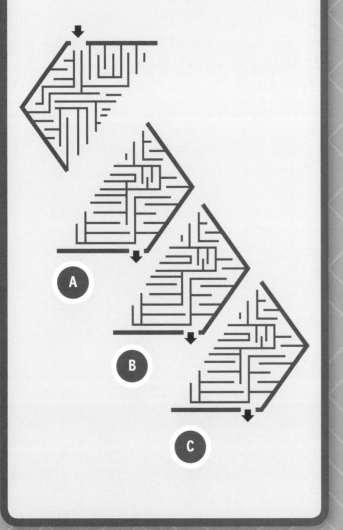

A

B

C

Shape Shift

GENIUS GENUS: SPATIAL SUPERSTAR

Move three pieces to transform image A into image B.

IMAGE A

IMAGE B

Having trouble? Cut out pieces of paper in these shapes to arrange and solve.

Test Your S.M.A.R.T.S.!

(SUPERIOR MENTAL ACUITY AND RATIONALITY TESTING SYSTEM)

WELL, WELL ... YOU'VE MADE IT MORE THAN HALFWAY THROUGH THE BOOK. Why, I bet if your muscular mind looked in a mirror, it would hardly recognize itself!

I think you may be just the Mastermind I'm looking for. That means I need to get serious about crafting cranium challenges. Let's see what you've got!

1. The spatial reasoning you use to catch a baseball and throw it to second base involves these two parts of your brain:

- **P** motor cortex and neurons
- **R** visual cortex and sensory cortex
- **T** parietal cortex and hippocampus
- **A** humor center and laugh cortex

Hidden Word: ___ ___ ___ ___ ___

2. Alan Burgess's condition, hemispatial neglect, makes his brain:

S ignore everything on his left side

E send too much visual information from his eyes to his brain

I lose his balance so that he falls over

D be very good at drawing

Hidden Word: ____ ____ ____ ____

3. What do cats use to help them get around in the dark?

A Their fur

D Their tails

R Their whiskers

K Tiny GPS units

Hidden Word: ____ ____ ____ ____

4. Most people have one type of spatial genius: they are either _____ or _____.

C Trunk Packers, Navigators

P puzzle solvers, readers

K artists, engineers

A squirrels, taxi drivers

Hidden Word: ____ ____ ____ ____

RECORD YOUR ANSWERS HERE

1 2 3 4

YOU ARE HERE

Watch out! Walking encyclopedia coming through

Budding egghead

You're pretty intelligent ... for a primate

Bet you can outwit Atom

Slightly smarter than you were an hour ago

Not a total blockhead

MASTERMIND METER

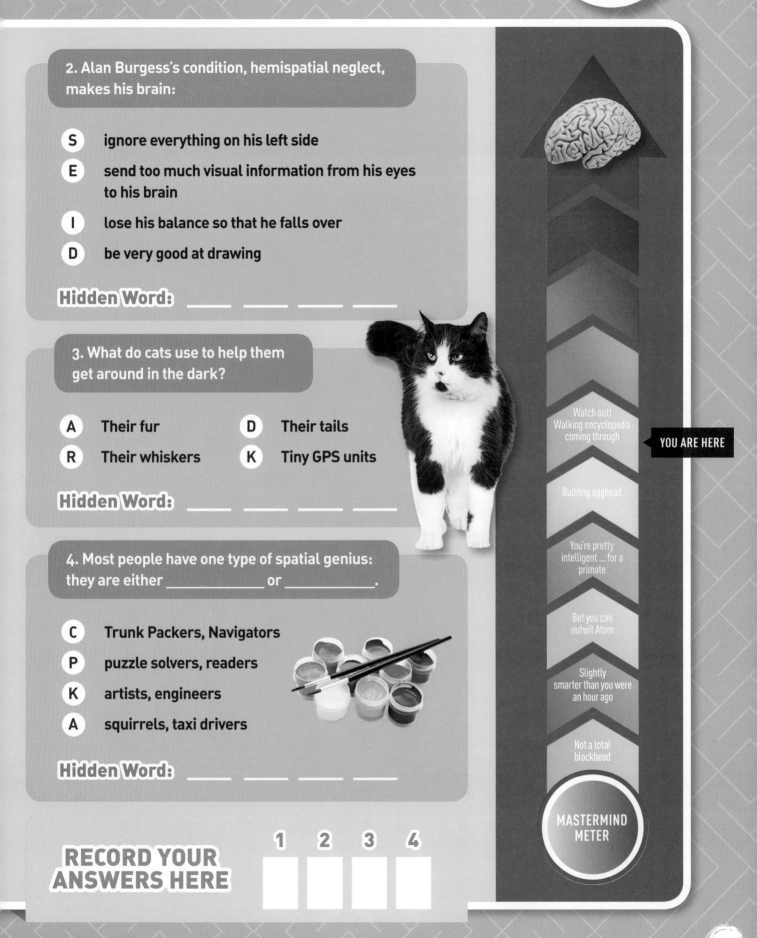

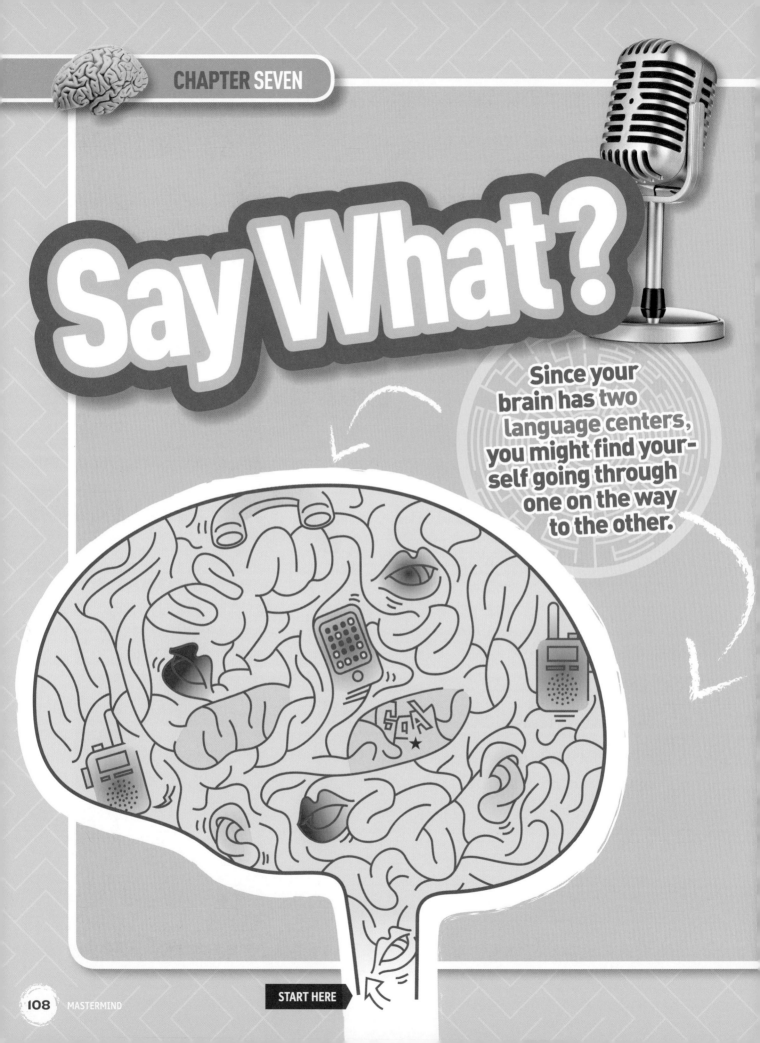

CHAPTER SEVEN

Say What?

Since your brain has two language centers, you might find yourself going through one on the way to the other.

START HERE

You're feeling pretty good about your bulked-up brainpower, aren't you? Well, how about a little challenge? Consider this sentence: **The vingo binks glorphed the naphavore.** It's just silly nonsense, right? Yes and no. Answer me this: Would you rather be the vingo binks or the naphavore?

Although these words don't mean anything, the sentence does. Most people can say without hesitating that they'd rather be the vingo binks. They'd rather be doing the glorphing than being glorphed, whatever that is!

Your brain uses patterns to understand language. Your pattern detector is so skillful that you can get meaning from language even if you don't understand the words—like in the example above. Listen up to learn more!

How It Works

1

When you speak or write words, you are using a part of your brain called **Broca's area.** People with damage to this area can understand words perfectly well, but they can't speak.

2

When you listen to and understand words, you are using a part of your brain called **Wernicke's area.** Wernicke's area helps you recognize patterns—it's how you figured out the meaning of the nonsense sentence on the last page.

3

When you have a conversation with someone, Broca's and Wernicke's areas work together to help you both talk and listen.

IMA GENIUS'S BRAINIAC BONUS: **CROSSED WORDS**

There are nine hints below, each describing a single word.
The hints are grouped by whether the word will go on the grid
horizontally (left to right) or vertically (top to bottom)
but are not otherwise in any particular order. One letter
has been placed on the grid for you.

HORIZONTAL (5 letters each)

- What one does to a door when angry
- Focus of this book
- Major artery
- Nightly activity

VERTICAL (4 letters each)

- What a baby does several times a day
- A section or place
- Yummy dinner bread
- One on a list
- Treble's opposite

B				

ATOM'S **BRAIN BREAK**

The toughest tongue twister in the world is:

"The sixth sick sheik's sixth sheep's sick."

Try it!

FUN FACT
Humans are wired for language. Newborn babies can already tell the difference between the sounds "b" and "p."

TiME TRIALS

It's time to test your mental speed! Grab a pencil and see how fast you can complete these puzzles.

Thanks to your Broca's and Wernicke's areas, this unexpected condition occurs worldwide. **Use the cypher below to decode the secret message.**

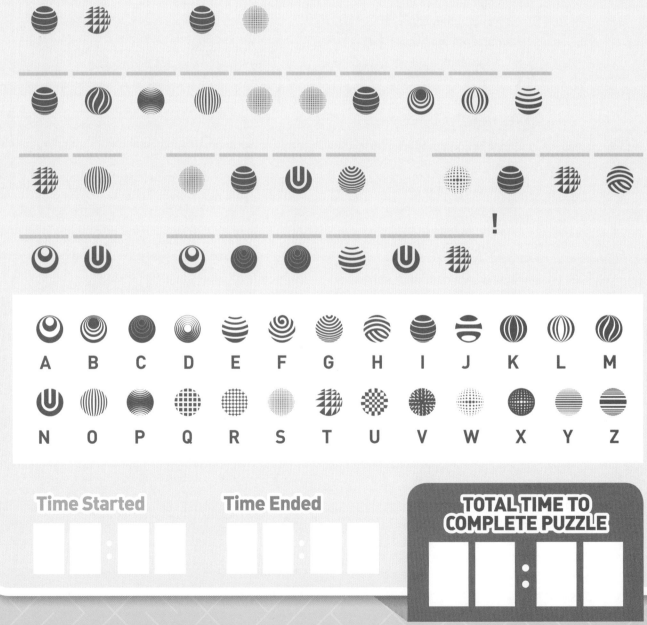

Time Started

Time Ended

TOTAL TIME TO COMPLETE PUZZLE

Animals don't talk to each other ... or do they? Find your way to the end of the question mark—and onto the next page—for some answers!

START HERE

GOAL ★

Time Started

☐☐ : ☐☐

Time Ended

☐☐ : ☐☐

TOTAL TIME TO COMPLETE PUZZLE

☐☐ : ☐☐

Communicating Critters

YOU HUMANS AREN'T THE ONLY TALKING CREATURES ON EARTH! We animals may not use words, but we still get the point across.

FUN FACT

Termites might look like tiny ants, but they are actually a species of cockroach.

THUMPING BUGS

African termites build giant mounds out of dirt. The termites live inside the dirt mounds. If a predator, like the long-tongued aardvark, comes close, termite soldiers use head banging to sound the alarm.

No, it's not a rock concert! The soldier termites bang their heads on the ground about 11 times a second. The sound only travels a few inches (cm), but any termites close enough to hear start head banging, too. Using this chain-reaction communication, termites let the whole colony know danger is close. Now that's using your head!

COLORFUL **CHATTER**

Caribbean reef squid can change the colors and patterns on their skin in the blink of an eye—what a nifty trick! This ability isn't only good for hiding from hungry predators; the squid use their color changes to communicate!

A male squid attracts a female by putting on a stripe pattern that says, "Hey, pretty lady." If he sees another male, he'll change to a splotchy pattern that says, "Go away! I'm tougher than you!"

The squid can even say two things at once: If he has a female on his right and another male on his left, he will make his body striped on the right side and splotchy on the left. Talk about a mixed message!

DANCING WITH **BEES**

A forager bee's job is to find food for the whole hive. But once a forager locates some tasty nectar, how does it tell the other bees how to get there?

When the forager gets back to the nest, it enters a special "dance floor" area of the hive. Now it's time to show off some moves! The forager dances in a figure eight pattern while the other bees watch. Using this "waggle dance," the bee can tell its bee friends which direction they need to go to find food, and how far they'll have to fly to get there.

It can even use its dancing to describe how tasty the food is! A super-energetic dance tells the other bees that the nectar is rich and delicious.

HOLD THE **PHONE**

Just like you and your friends, dolphins work in teams to accomplish tasks. Also like you, they talk to each other to do it. Starting from birth, dolphins squeak, squawk, click, and whistle. They also use body language to talk to each other, changing their postures, clapping their jaws, and blowing bubbles.

Scientists have been trying to crack the code to dolphin language, but they still don't know what these smarty-pants mammals are saying. One thing is clear: They're definitely talking to each other.

In one experiment, scientists put a mother and baby dolphin into separate tanks. The pair were still able to communicate ... over the telephone! The tanks were connected by a special audio link. The pair made chirping and squawking noises back and forth. Maybe they were asking, "How's the water over there?"

Bubble Trouble

GENIUS
GENUS:
WORD
WIZARD

What did the mother dolphin say to her young dolphin during dinner?

Rearrange the bubbles to reveal her message.

____ _____ _____ __ ____ _____

UR

WA

OP

OW

BB

IN

ING

BL

BU

TER

YO

ST

LES

Those were some clever creatures on the last page! Can you use your hefty human brain to solve these puzzles?

Spreading the Word

These two colonies of African termites are exactly the same in size and shape. Each circle is a termite, and the red one is the messenger. The only difference between these two colonies is where each messenger stands when delivering the message. Messages spread out to the nearest termites, which must in turn pass on the message to their nearest termites, without skipping over any termites.

If the messengers deliver their messages at the same time, which colony will be completely informed first?

Bee Dance

Four bees have returned to the hive after searching for nectar. Each bee performs a waggle dance, telling the other bees about what she has found. I've deciphered each of their dances for you below. Based on the information these four bees have given, which bee's dance will the colony use to find nectar?

THE DANCES:

Anna Bee's dance describes sweet nectar that is two miles (3.2 km) away. The bees will have to fly a long way, but the nectar is sweet, sweet, sweet!

Babs Bee's dance tells of flowers with sweet and slightly tart, earthy-flavored nectar to the northeast. The bees will find tons of flowers bearing nectar!

Clara Bee's dance tells of a slightly sweet honey that the bees will enjoy, but they will have to fly south for six miles (10 km)!

Suzie Bee's dance reveals a super-sweet honey directly to the west. From Suzie Bee's excitement, this batch of nectar is extremely sweet!

GENIUS GENUS: LOGICAL LEADER

The Woman With Two Brains

VICKI IS STANDING IN FRONT OF HER CLOSET PICKING OUT HER OUTFIT FOR THE DAY. She decides that she wants to wear a blue sweater. She reaches for it with her right hand. But at the same time, her left hand comes up and grabs a red shirt. It's like each hand has a mind of its own!

Vicki is a **split-brain** patient. When she was younger, she suffered from dangerous seizures. To make them stop, surgeons cut her **corpus callosum,** the bundle of nerves that connects the two halves of her brain. The surgery probably saved her life. But it left the two halves of her brain with no way to talk to each other.

Language is tough for split-brain patients like Vicki. That's because Vicki's language center is on the left side of her brain. When surgeons cut the connection between her brain's two sides, the right side could no longer access her language center.

Using a special screen, scientists can show a picture of a dog to only Vicki's left eye. When they ask Vicki what she sees, she says, "Nothing." That's because her left eye sends the image to her right brain, which can no longer use language. Even though both Vicki's eyes work perfectly, she can't say what she's seeing.

But if scientists then put a pencil in Vicki's left hand, and ask her to draw what she sees, she draws a picture of a dog with no trouble. Her right brain sees the dog—it just can't say so. What a mental mix-up!

Lefty Lingo

Are you right-handed, or left-handed? In almost 100 percent of righties, the left side of the brain controls language. But in lefties, language is often controlled by both sides of the brain, or even totally by the right side.

Remember how the right side of your brain controls the left side of your body and vice versa? Left-handed people can be better at certain things tied to the right side of the brain, like math, spatial reasoning, and art. They also may use language in slightly different ways than their right-handed buddies. That's lefty ... I mean nifty!

MYTHS
BUSTED!

MYTH: A penny dropped from the Empire State Building could kill someone.

BUSTED!: A falling penny's top speed is 30 to 50 miles an hour (48 to 81 km/h). It won't go any faster than that, no matter how far it falls. And since the Empire State Building is thicker on the bottom and skinnier on the top, it's impossible to drop anything directly from the top to street level, anyway.

Humans are naturally talented with language. But that doesn't mean these puzzles are easy! Are you up for the challenge?

The Stroop Effect

Look at the list below. Say the colors of the words out loud.
For example, if you see brown, you should say "pink."

RED

BLUE

GREEN

YELLOW

PURPLE

BLACK

ORANGE

If you stumbled your way through, or read the word instead of stating the color, then you've experienced the Stroop Effect! The Stroop Effect happens because the brain is so good at language. We recognize the letters before we process what color they are. That makes it tough to say the color instead!

Now take a piece of paper or a ruler, or even use your hand, and cover the left half of the list so the beginning of each word is hidden. State the colors of the list again. You will find that it's much easier! Your brain is no longer distracted by the words and can focus on the colors.

Body Lingo

Words are only one part of language. We use body language, or gestures and movements, to communicate, too. Use your body language smarts to match the emotions with the people below.

Draw a line from each person to the most appropriate emotion.

Doubtful Interested Defensive Lost in Thought Ready Nervous Not Confident Confident Truthful Bored

Out of the Box

Are you ready for some tricky puzzles? These riddles require you to think outside the box. Examine each word, and try to think of other ways it may be used.

1) The police told the adult to move away from the saw, so the kids could play with it. Where are they?

2) When the dog sits on a railroad, his owner's friend receives money. What is the friend doing?

3) Mr. Martin and Miss Duncan have finished building the tallest building in the city. Just as everyone was cheering this great accomplishment, a dog came along and with one swipe of its tail destroyed the building. How could this happen?

GENIUS GENUS: CREATIVITY CHAMPION

Back for more, I see! If you keep going at this rate, your brain is going to get too big for your skull! Just kidding—that's impossible.

Deceptive Design

Some designers like to turn ordinary items, such as a staircase banister, into a piece of art by hiding a picture or message inside. What do you see when you look at this banister?

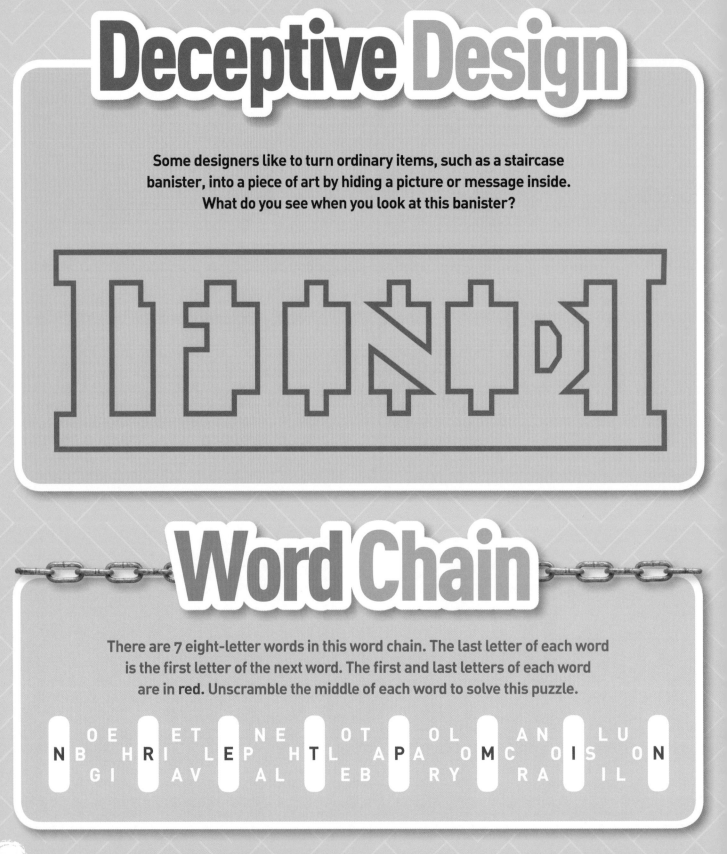

Word Chain

There are 7 eight-letter words in this word chain. The last letter of each word is the first letter of the next word. The first and last letters of each word are in **red**. Unscramble the middle of each word to solve this puzzle.

```
     OE    ET    NE     OT    OL    AN     LU
  N     HRI   EP     TL   APA  MC    IS    N
  B        L    H         A    O     O     O
  GI    AV    AL    EB     RY    RA    IL
```

Coordinated

GENIUS GENUS: LOGICAL LEADER

Complete the puzzle to reveal a secret message.

A	(a,7)	(b,3)	(b,6)	(c,3)	(c,4)
B	(c,8)				
E	(a,5)	(b,5)	(d,I)	(d,2)	(e,I) (e,6)
F	(b,7)				
G	(b,I)	(b,4)	(d,4)		
H	(a,4)				
I	(a,I)	(c,I)			
K	(c,2)				
L	(a,6)				

M	(e,2)	(e,7)	
N	(a,2)	(a,8)	(c,5)
O	(d,5)	(d,8)	(e,5)
R	(b,8)		
S	(c,6)	(d,3)	
T	(a,3)		
U	(b,2)		
Z	(d,7)	(e,4)	

	1	2	3	4	5	6	7	8
a								
b								
c							,	
d						"		
e			,					"

GENIUS GENUS: WORD WIZARD

Mess of a Story

A husband sent this text to his wife. Unfortunately, he types so fast that he often types letters out of order. Can you deduce what he is saying? We've added hints below his scrambled words.

While driving and looking for the **LOUD TAN RAM,** we saw a large **A MOTH VESSEL** flipped over on its side,
(place to clean clothes) *(construction vehicle)*

trapping the driver. A **LOW IMP CANOE** came over to help, but too many **PET SARDINES** were in the way.
(law enforcement officer) *(people who cross a street)*

The **CAMPER AIDS** got there in plenty of time to take the driver to the **HALO PITS**
(first aid workers) *(medical building)*

Test Your S.M.A.R.T.S.!

(SUPERIOR MENTAL ACUITY AND RATIONALITY TESTING SYSTEM)

MY LAB TESTS SHOW THAT YOU'RE GETTING SMARTER WITH EVERY PAGE. I see that I have finally found a worthy brain to take ove— Err, never mind. Let's keep going!

You'd better put on your thinking cap, because if you want to make it all the way to Mastermind status, you'll have to carry on with one mental challenge after another ... Speaking of—see if you can still solve my bonus challenge, finding the hidden words.

1. Your brain's Broca's area helps you _____.

E   sleep

R   run

A   speak or write words

A   listen to and understand words

Hidden Word: ___ ___ ___ ___ ___

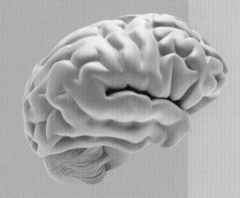

2. Your brain's Wernicke's area helps you _____.

- **W** listen to and understand words
- **D** speak or write words
- **R** eat
- **O** sit quietly

Hidden Word: ____ ____ ____ ____ ____

3. What does a honeybee's "waggle dance" tell the other bees in the hive?

- **E** When the sun will rise
- **H** What the weather is like
- **V** Directions to find food
- **I** What kind of music the bee likes

Hidden Word: ____ ____ ____

4. The _____ is the bundle of nerves that connects the two halves of the brain.

- **I** corpus callosum
- **N** hippocampus
- **J** frontal cortex
- **O** neuron

Hidden Word: ____ ____ ____ ____

RECORD YOUR ANSWERS HERE

1	2	3	4

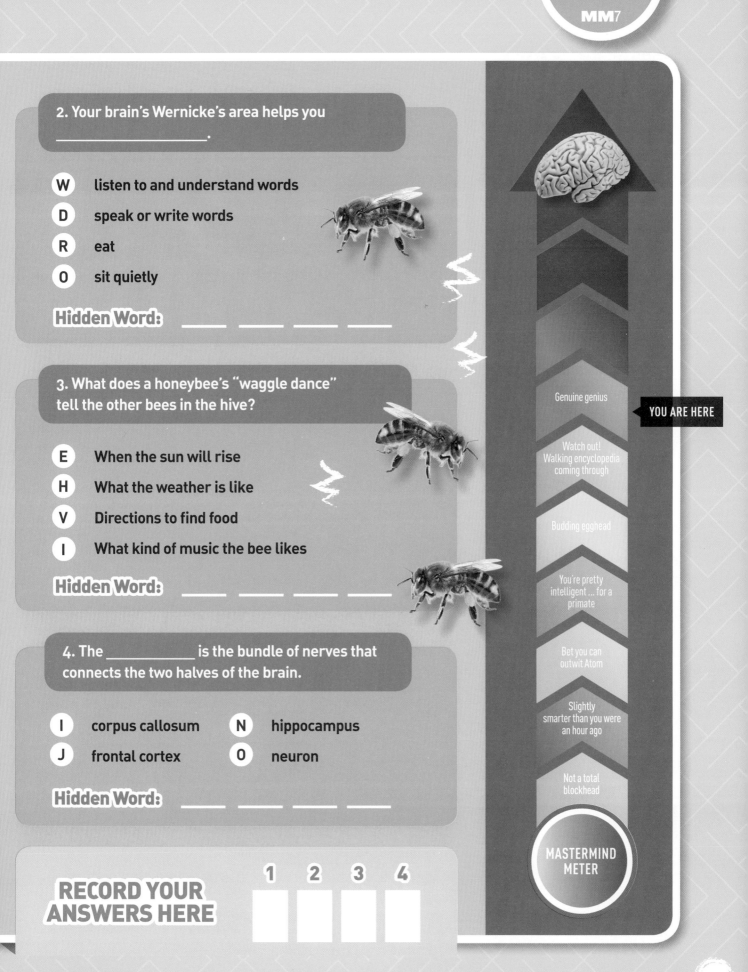

YOU ARE HERE

Genuine genius

Watch out! Walking encyclopedia coming through

Budding egghead

You're pretty intelligent ... for a primate

Bet you can outwit Atom

Slightly smarter than you were an hour ago

Not a total blockhead

MASTERMIND METER

CHAPTER EIGHT

Where's My Homework?

Perhaps you will remember how to find your way from the frontal cortex to the hippo-campus.

START HERE

Wow, you've made it all the way to chapter 8!

I bet you remember every single thing you've learned so far, right? Ha! Didn't think so.

Have you ever wondered why you can remember some events forever, like the time you won first place at the track meet? So why do other memories—like where you put your homework—slip away right when you need them?

We use our memories all day, every day. They help us remember to check for traffic before crossing the street, tie our shoelaces, and ace that math test.

Without your memory, you wouldn't be you. But memory isn't perfect. In fact, sometimes what you remember isn't the truth at all!

How It Works

1

Your **short-term memory** holds on to a small piece of information for a short amount of time. These memories are stored in the **frontal cortex.** The brain can keep seven digits in its short-term memory for about 20–30 seconds. You use your short-term memory when you see a phone number on a billboard and remember it just long enough to dial.

2

To change a short-term memory into a long-term memory, the brain sends it to the **hippocampus.** Long-term memories stay in your brain forever. For example, you don't ever have to ask your mom what time your favorite TV show comes on, because you've stored the start time in your long-term memory.

3

Long-term memories make permanent changes in your brain. To create them, your brain strengthens the connections between certain neurons, like the ones that make you hungry for pizza and the ones that store the name of your favorite pizza delivery place.

MYTHS
BUSTED!

MYTH: Goldfish have a three-second memory.

BUSTED!: Goldfish are actually quite smart. Studies show that they can be trained to perform simple tricks, which definitely requires more than three seconds of memory.

4

Long-term memories aren't kept in any one single place in your brain. Instead, they are stored in the connections between neurons all over your noggin. Your brain can never "fill up" with memories—your connections will just get stronger and stronger the more you learn. So keep at it!

ATOM'S **BRAIN BREAK**

Some lipsticks contain fish scales. What a **fishy** trick!

TiME TRiALS

You know what to do—it's Time Trial time. See if you can beat your times from the last chapter!

Remembering can be tricky. Discover how your arms and legs can help you!
Use the cypher below to decode the secret message.

(Decoded message: EXERCISE HELPS YOUR BRAIN MAKE MEMORIES)

A	B	C	D	E	F	G	H	I	J	K	L	M
✏️	👓	frog	spider	turtle	key	planet	arrow	paintbrush	spray	turtle	truck	baby

N	O	P	Q	R	S	T	U	V	W	X	Y	Z
face	face	hand	—∤	—‖	∿	anchor	firecracker	mitten	clover	cross	bandage	dog

Time Started

Time Ended

TOTAL TIME TO COMPLETE PUZZLE

It's time to leave for school, but where's your jacket? Can you remember where you put it? Enter the time you start and the time you finish.

START HERE

Time Started

Time Ended

TOTAL TIME TO COMPLETE PUZZLE

Memory Lies

HAVE YOU EVER HAD A MEMORY FROM YOUR EARLY CHILDHOOD THAT YOU AND YOUR PARENTS REMEMBER DIFFERENTLY? Before you go telling them they're wrong, take note: When it comes to believing everything you see or hear, sometimes you can't trust your own noggin.

You see, every time you think of a memory, your brain might change a detail or two. Like the taste of the cake at your sixth birthday party: Over the years, you might remember it as vanilla, then strawberry, then chocolate. And the whole time, you're convinced you remember the right flavor! Calling up memories makes them more permanent, but it can also tweak the details and make them less true.

Consider this: In one experiment, scientists showed people a video of a car crash and then asked them questions about it. Just by changing the wording of their questions, the scientists were able to alter peoples' memories of what they had seen. When the scientists asked how fast the cars were going when they "hit" each other, the average person said 34 miles an hour (55 km/h). When the scientists asked how fast the cars were going when they "smashed into" each other, the average person said 41 miles an hour (66 km/h).

For this reason, eyewitnesses—like people who see a car crash from the sidewalk—sometimes remember things differently from how they actually happened. Eyewitness testimony has been used in courtrooms for a long time. But that is now changing as scientists learn that our memories aren't totally trustworthy.

IMA GENIUS'S BRAINIAC BONUS: **BACKTRACKING**

Sally took a hike up the mountain. She started at 8 a.m. and kept a steady pace the entire way. Unfortunately, she dropped her water bottle during the hike and had to go back down the path until she found it. Once Sally found the bottle, she continued hiking up the mountain and finally arrived at the top at 2 p.m.

After two hours of taking photos and writing in her science journal about the plants, Sally headed down the mountain, walking at the same pace and taking the same path as before. She arrived at the bottom of the mountain, at her original starting point, at 8 p.m.

How long did it take Sally to find her water bottle once she realized she had lost it?

Smelling Sensation

Have you ever noticed that certain smells can bring back vivid memories and moods? The smell of chlorine, for example, might make you feel excited, making you remember summer days you spent at the pool. The smell of baking cookies might remind you of Grandma, and make you feel safe and happy.

Scientists think smells may evoke memories and emotions because of how your brain is laid out. The area of your brain that processes smells is close to both the **amygdala,** which processes emotion, and the **hippocampus,** where long-term memories are formed. That means smells, memories, and emotions are tightly linked in your brain.

It's in the Details

Your own memory lies to you all the time—the nerve! Want proof? Try this puzzle.

This puzzle has five steps. They must be done in order. To start, read the story below. Then proceed to step two.

STEP ONE   Read the story:

On his way home from practice, Michael realized he had left his blue sweater in the team's locker room. He raced back on his bicycle and luckily found the sweater on a bench. He would have been in trouble had he lost that sweater! His grandmother had spent a lot of time in her rocking chair, making the sweater for him by hand. Hoping he wouldn't be late for dinner, Michael zipped past the bakery. He couldn't resist buying some delicious baked goods. He chomped down a yummy chocolate treat then hopped back onto his bicycle and raced home. As he walked in the door and heard his mom call him, Michael quickly wiped his mouth so she wouldn't know what he had been up to. He dropped his backpack, washed up, and joined the family just in time for dinner.

STEP TWO

Turn the book upside down and read the instructions on the opposite page.

Whoo! I'm getting dizzy!

STEP THREE

Close your eyes and count to 20. Then try to remember as many details as you can about the story. Do NOT reread any part of the story, or you won't be able to complete the puzzle correctly!

Ready ... set ... go!

STEP FOUR

Great, by now you've remembered every detail of the story, right?

Let's see just how reliable your memory is. Answer the questions below.

1. What color eyes does Michael have? _____

2. What sport does Michael play? _____

3. Did Michael's grandmother knit or sew the sweater for him? _____

4. Did Michael eat a cookie at the bakery? _____

5. Was his bicycle a road bike or mountain bike? _____

STEP FIVE

Don't return to the story to check your answers, you won't find them there. This is not your normal puzzle & solution activity.

Check the solution on page 172 to find out what's going on!

The Man Who Can't Remember

JIMMIE G. WAS A TALKATIVE AND FRIENDLY 49-YEAR-OLD MAN WHO COULD BEAT HIS DOCTOR EASILY AT CHECKERS AND DO ARITHMETIC WITH AMAZING SPEED. But when the doctor showed him a picture of Earth taken from space, Jimmie was stunned. "Doc, you're kidding! Someone would've had to get a camera up there!" he said. The picture was taken by astronauts during the 1969 moon landing. Even though Jimmie had lived through this famous event, he didn't remember it.

When his doctor asked him how old he was, Jimmie said, "Nineteen." In his mind, time had stopped in 1945! His doctor held up a mirror and showed Jimmie his reflection—a white-haired, middle-aged man. Jimmie was confused and terrified.

Jimmie had **anterograde amnesia.** People with this type of amnesia cannot change **short-term memories** into **long-term memories.** Jimmie could use his short-term memory to carry on a conversation with someone perfectly well. But if the person left the room and came back a few minutes later, Jimmie G. would introduce himself again. He didn't remember ever meeting the person, because he had formed no long-term memories of the event.

Because scientists don't completely understand how memories are formed, amnesia is a mysterious disease. For one thing, it only affects some types of memory. When scientists gave Jimmie the same maze to complete every morning, he got faster at doing it each time—even though he didn't remember ever seeing it before. Talk about a memory mystery!

FUN FACT

Dory, the forgetful blue fish from the movie *Finding Nemo*, has anterograde amnesia, just like Jimmie G!

The Woman Who Can't Forget

Jimmie G. can't remember anything for long. But Jill Price has the opposite problem: She can't forget anything! Jill has a condition called **hyperthymesia.** She can remember every detail of every day she's lived since she was 14.

Price says that her daily life is "like a split screen." On one side, she sees the present; on the other side, she sees detailed memories from her past. Unlike most people, she can remember specific things about routine days, like what she had for lunch or whether it was cloudy.

Ask her about August 16, 1977, and she'll tell you, "It was a Tuesday. Elvis died." May 18, 1980? "A Sunday. Mount St. Helens erupted."

It isn't always easy for Price to live with her condition. Sometimes she gets comfort from good memories from long ago. But she can also never forget the times she's made a bad decision, hurt someone, or been embarrassed. All the events of her life, both good and bad, are with her forever. Would you want to never forget?

I think these memory puzzles may be my trickiest yet. Will your newfound brainpower be enough?

Face It

Remembering names can be hard. If you can find something about a person to associate with his or her name, you'll improve your chances of recalling it the next time you meet.

If you look at Chester here, you could say he's rather cheery.
Let's call him Cheery Chester.

Below are five people. For each person, use the first letter of the person's name to try to find a word that describes something about that person (clothing, feature, job, activity, personality, or expression) that starts with that letter. The word can come before or after the person's name.

TED
....
BETTY
....
PAMELA
....
SAM
....
LARRY
....

It's a Jumble

PART ONE

Take only five seconds to memorize the words below, then quickly turn the page.

00:05

BIKE
RAKE
HEIGHT
HIKE
BAKE
RIGHT

HINT: Grouping words that sound alike will help make you a memory master.

Locker Layout

PART ONE

Look at the items in the locker below. Try to memorize as much detail as you can. Then, turn the page for the second part of the puzzle.

It's a Rainbow

Good work, savvy student! Now see if you can get these brain-twisting challenges right!

Create a sentence to remember the colors of the rainbow. The words should start with the same first letter of each color, in order. There is no right or wrong answer. The challenge is seeing how creative you can be.

Here are the colors in order: Red, Orange, Yellow, Green, Blue, Indigo, Violet

There are many **mnemonics** you can create, and they don't have to be true or even make much sense, as long as they make the list easier for YOU to remember! Some well-known mnemonics for the rainbow include:

A NAME: ROY G. BIV   **A SENTENCE:** Richard Of York Gave Battle In Vain

We decided to make up our own super-silly mnemonic. The stranger or sillier a mnemonic is, the easier it is for your brain to remember:

Roaches On Yachts Gargle Bubbly, Icy Vomit

Hand-y Trick

It can be tricky to remember your left from your right. Here are two easy mnemonic devices to help you never get them mixed up again.

1) If you place the words LEFT and RIGHT in alphabetical order, LEFT will be on the left, and RIGHT with be on the right.

2) If you lay your two hands out in front of you, with the four fingers together and the thumb stretched far away, only one hand makes the shape of the letter "L," and that's your left hand.

LEFT

It's a Jumble

PART TWO

Now that you've memorized the words on the previous page, you should have no trouble recalling them, right?

What were the words?

1.

2.

3.

4.

5.

6.

Hey, Mastermind, what kind of dog makes the best scientist? A laboratory retriever. Ha! Get it? I crack myself up!

Locker Layout

PART TWO

The student who owns this locker stopped by in the short space of time that you were memorizing the locker's contents (fast kid, right?). Some items have been added, moved, or removed. Circle any new or moved items. Now here's the really tricky part … Can you list the six items that are missing?

_____   _____
_____   _____
_____   _____

Test Your S.M.A.R.T.S.!

(SUPERIOR MENTAL ACUITY AND RATIONALITY TESTING SYSTEM)

THE HUMAN BRAIN CAN REMEMBER AN AMAZING AMOUNT OF INFORMATION! After all these chapters, even *your* brain is bulked up with beautiful facts! I can't wait to get my hands on it ... Err, what was I saying?

Only one chapter stands between you and true Mastermind status. But beware ... That chapter might just be my most devious yet. First, tackle this quiz and bonus challenge ... if you dare!

1. Which type of memories are stored in the frontal cortex?

R   Long-term memories

M   Short-term memories

E   Neural memories

T   Future memories

Hidden Word: _____ _____ _____

2. How does your brain create new long-term memories?

- V   By deleting old long-term memories
- E   By combining short-term memories together
- I   By replaying short-term memories over and over
- G   By strengthening connections between neurons

Hidden Word: ____ ____ ____ ____

3. Someone with _____, like Jimmie G., can't make new long-term memories.

- E   anterograde amnesia
- K   hypothymesia
- M   hemispatial neglect
- A   forgetfulness syndrome

Hidden Word: ____ ____ ____ ____

4. Someone with hyperthymesia, like Jill Price, _____.

- P   can't make new memories
- E   can't forget anything
- K   always gets lost
- F   remembers things that didn't happen

Hidden Word: ____ ____ ____ ____

RECORD YOUR ANSWERS HERE

1 2 3 4

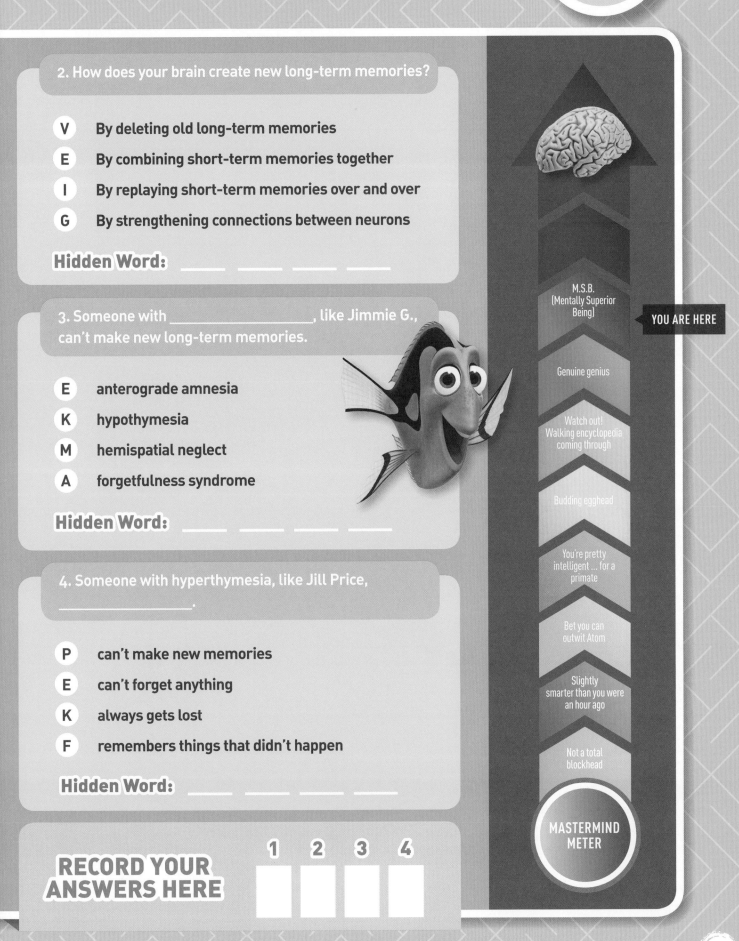

YOU ARE HERE

M.S.B. (Mentally Superior Being)

Genuine genius

Watch out! Walking encyclopedia coming through

Budding egghead

You're pretty intelligent ... for a primate

Bet you can outwit Atom

Slightly smarter than you were an hour ago

Not a total blockhead

MASTERMIND METER

CHAPTER NINE

Figure It Out

Can you puzzle your way through the brain to the frontal cortex?

GOAL

START HERE

Question: What sound do porcupines make when they kiss?

Answer: Ouch!

Humans love jokes. But have you ever stopped to wonder why?

Our brains are really good at following patterns—so good that we are always predicting what's coming next, without even thinking about it. When you think about two porcupines kissing, your brain expects a smooching noise (Eww!). But then you hear the punch line, and it's totally different: "Ouch!" Your brain didn't expect that answer. That makes it funny!

The ability to follow patterns makes humans good at solving problems. Jokes outsmart our problem-solving skills. But most of the time, these skills are pretty impressive. We use problem solving every day. In fact, I'll be using mine very soon to take over your brai— Oops, I mean, turn the page to find out how!

How It Works

1

Here's a puzzler: Think of a word that goes with all three of these words: "tooth," "heart," and "potato."

2

There are two ways your brain solves problems. One is called **trial-and-error** problem solving. It works by testing possible solutions one at a time: something like this.

Let's see, what goes with "tooth"? How about "ache"? "Toothache, heartache ... potatoache?" Uh oh. That can't be it ...

Hmm ... tooth, heart, potato ... I know, "sweet"! "Sweet tooth, sweetheart, sweet potato!"

3

Then there's another kind of problem solving—**insight** problem solving. When you use insight problem solving, your brain explores lots of possible solutions all at the same time. You're not aware of the process—the answer just seems to come to you.

Funny Thoughts

It's hard to solve certain kinds of puzzles—like the one on the opposite page—using trial-and-error problem solving. It would take your brain a long time to test every word there is until it lands on "sweet."

For this type of puzzle, insight problem solving works much better. But once your brain starts doing trial-and-error, it can't go back to insight problem solving. How stubborn!

One group of scientists has found a way to encourage your brain to solve problems by insight—making you laugh! The scientists showed one group of people videos of stand-up comedy. They showed another group scary movies. Then they gave both groups three-word puzzles (like the one on the left) to solve. The people who had just watched comedy were better at finding the answers!

This study tells us that being in a good mood may help us be more creative. And being anxious may make it harder to solve problems. So the next time you're stuck on a homework problem, don't stress. Instead, try watching a quick video that makes you laugh or turning on your favorite song and dancing like crazy. If anyone asks what you're doing, say, "I'm thinking, of course!"

ATOM'S BRAIN BREAK

The average person eats about one pound (0.45 kg) of insects each year!

TiME TRiALS

This is it—the last set of Time Trials! Give these puzzles all you've got. Then look back at all the Time Trials you've completed throughout this book. Have your times gotten faster since the beginning chapters? That's because your brain has gotten stronger!

You need logic and insight to solve many puzzles, especially cryptograms. Good luck!
Use the cypher below to decode the secret message.

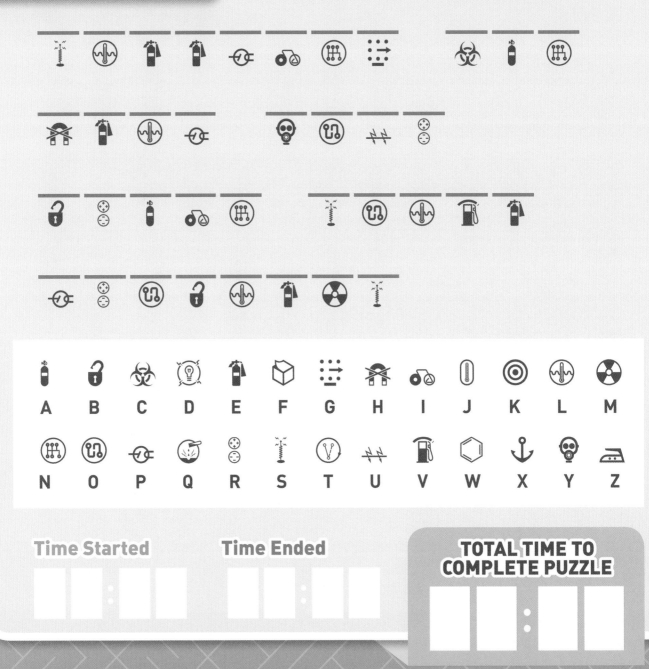

Time Started

Time Ended

TOTAL TIME TO COMPLETE PUZZLE

To find the solution to a problem, you may need to think outside the box. Enter the time you start and the time you finish.

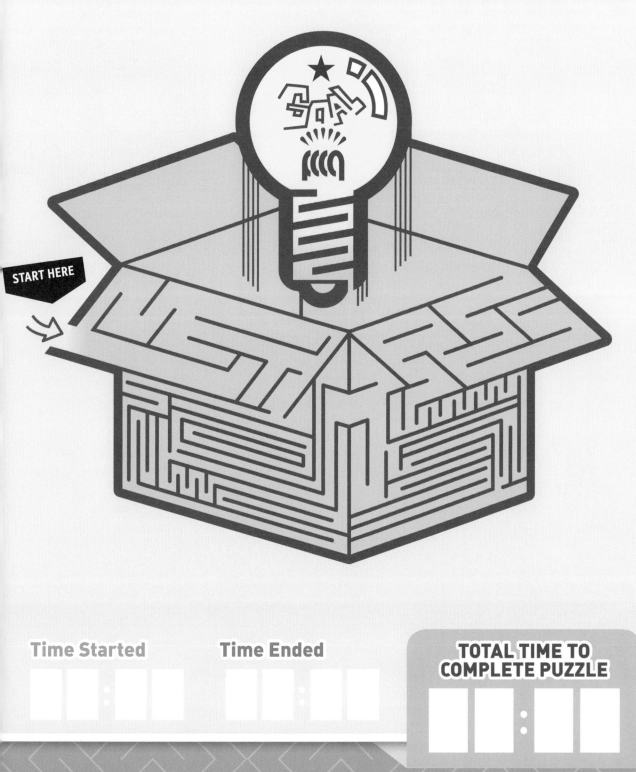

START HERE

Time Started

Time Ended

TOTAL TIME TO COMPLETE PUZZLE

Animal Geniuses

YOU'VE READ ABOUT LOTS OF SMART CREATURES IN THESE PAGES. But these problem solvers just may be the brainiest animals on the planet (besides me, of course)!

TANK TRICKS

Can you juggle? It's a tricky skill. I myself have a hard time juggling, since I don't have thumbs. But it isn't too tricky for Otto the octopus. Otto, who lives at the Sea Star Aquarium in Germany, has been spotted juggling the hermit crabs that share his tank!

That's not Otto's only smart skill. Once, the octopus became annoyed with a bright light shining into his aquarium. He climbed onto the rim of tank and sprayed a jet of water at the light until—*sizzle*—it shorted out. The aquarium staff couldn't figure out what was causing the blackouts. They had to take turns sleeping on the floor until they caught Otto in the act!

Octopuses may be some of the world's greatest problem solvers. In the wild, they climb into lobster traps to steal the tasty crustaceans inside and then sneak back out unharmed. In captivity, they have been known to slip out of their tanks at night and climb into other ones to feast on fish, then sneak back home. If it weren't for the wet trails they leave on the floor, they would never get caught!

ELEMENTARY, MY DEAR **ELEPHANT**

Elephant brains are very similar to human brains. An elephant's cortex, the brain area associated with smarty-pants tasks like remembering, thought, and language, has the same number of neurons as a human's. What a brainy beast!

Scientists decided to put elephants' math skills to the test. They put two buckets in front of elephants at a Tokyo zoo. They dropped lots of apples into each bucket, making sure the elephants couldn't see inside. Then they asked the elephants to choose a bucket. Seventy-four percent of the time, the elephants chose the bucket with the most apples. They were able to keep count of how many apples were in each bucket as they were dropping. Not impressed? The average human only scored 67 percent on this task! Now if they had only asked me to try ...

APE ESCAPE

Did you know that you're an ape? No, I'm not calling you names, it's true! Humans are a type of ape, along with orangutans, chimpanzees, bonobos, and gorillas. All the creatures in this group are A+ animal smarties.

Of all the apes, orangutans are especially good at using tools to solve problems. They don't like rain, so to avoid getting wet, they'll make umbrellas out of leaves.

One orangutan named Fu Manchu kept getting out of his cage at the Omaha Zoo. He pried a wire off a light fixture and used it to pick the lock to his cage—just like an escaping human prisoner in the movies! In between breakouts, Fu Manchu would even sneakily store his lock pick in his mouth so he could escape whenever he wanted without being found out.

BIRDBRAIN

Crows love to eat tasty walnuts ... but have you ever tried to open one of those without a nut-cracker? It's tough! (Now try it using paws!) Crows are so smart that they've figured out a way to make humans do the nutcracking for them. These brainy birds have been spotted dropping the nuts in front of cars. When—*crunch!*—tires crack the shell, the crows swoop in to grab their snack.

But they make sure not to jaywalk—the crows wait until the light is red and the crosswalk sign is on, so they don't get run over! Now who are you calling birdbrain?

Word Camo

Just as animals can camouflage themselves, so too can words.
In the paragraph below, find 11 animals hiding in the story.
They are using the empty spaces between words to help them hide.

(For example: "anchor service" hides the word "horse"—anchor service.)

Tomato Adrift

When the limo used for transporting the president was seen hauling a magnetic rowboat to the pier, reporters became suspicious. This was no way to catch aliens who had stolen the president's bronze bracelet. Perhaps the military would forgo attacking the aliens. After all, they looked like tomatoes, and the president had fed them a subpar rotisserie chicken in tomato sauce, boathouse almonds, and broccoli onboard her yacht. And that is no way to treat guests, especially those who smell amazing even after bathing in tapioca melon pudding. What's next ... marzipan therapy?

After reading about these amazing animals, you might be feeling a little shaky in your status as Earth's superior brain. To take back your title, get both these puzzles right!

Beastly Phrases

GENIUS GENUS: LOGICAL LEADER

Figure out the meanings of these puzzles to prove how clever your human brain is.

Computer vs. Human

IN 2004, A RESEARCHER AT THE COMPUTER COMPANY IBM WAS EATING DINNER WHEN SUDDENLY, THE RESTAURANT FELL SILENT. The reason? Everyone was staring at the TV. They were watching a man named Ken Jennings compete on the trivia game show *Jeopardy!* Jennings won 74 straight games, the longest streak ever. That got the IBM researcher wondering ... Could he build a computer that could beat the *Jeopardy!* genius? Many experts thought it would be an impossible feat.

IBM built a computer named Watson. Watson's processors took up as much space as ten refrigerators. These processors could analyze the equivalent of a million books each second. Watson was going to be a tough competitor!

In February 2011, Watson and Jennings went head-to-head for two rounds of *Jeopardy!* Jennings was no match for the brilliant Watson. The computer correctly answered questions about geography, literature—even about an episode of *The Simpsons*! Watson won $1 million, proving that humans can build a machine smart enough ... to outsmart themselves! (Now if Watson only had a brain for me to study!)

MYTHS BUSTED!

MYTH: You only use 10 percent of your brain.

BUSTED!: People hooked up to brain-scanning technology show activity in all parts of the brain.

IMA GENIUS'S BRAINIAC BONUS: **CODEBREAKER**

You are a bona fide (that means real) Brainiac if you can break this code and reveal the message.

9	13	1

7	5	14	9	21	19

HINT:

16	21	26	26	12	5
P	U	Z	Z	L	E

Robot Takeover

Supersmart computers like Watson aren't just good for winning game shows. By the time you're a grown-up, humans and robots might interact all the time.

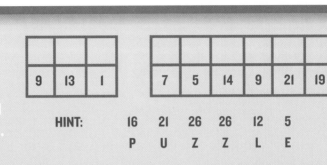

For example, engineers are currently working on a robot "doctor." RoboDoc will live on your wristwatch and give you basic medical advice whenever you need it. Some scientists predict that by sifting through all of the latest medical information, RoboDoc will be 99 percent accurate. But can RoboDoc replace your human doctor? The answer is no. When it comes to solving problems—like figuring out the best treatment for an illness—the human brain still reigns supreme. Scientists haven't been able to build a computer that works like the human mind.

Modern robots work by making basic yes-or-no choices. For example, scientists can teach a robot to get around a room by programming it to move away from anything it bumps into. That's no smarter than how a bug thinks. But this technology can still go far—in fact, it went all the way to Mars! It's the same programming that powers the Curiosity rover, the robot exploring the Red Planet right now.

Good work, student. I must say, way back in chapter 1, I never thought you'd make it this far! But I'm not quite done with you yet. These problem-solving puzzles might be the toughest of them all!

Letter Logic

Use your logic to determine where each letter belongs in the grid.
Use your insight to guess what sentence they're forming. The letters are listed below their correct column, but they may not be in order.

	O	R				A	N					T		E
O		L					A				H			
				O	T					L				.

C N U N	O R F I E	T P A I N
Y A N Y	B R G E N	I S A T H

Tricky Riddles

Some riddles require logic; others require thinking outside the box.
You might even need a combination for these puzzling riddles below.

1. A man named Joe walked into the store. He was drenched from head to toe. He plopped his sopping wet umbrella on the counter of the returns desk and demanded his money back.

Joe explained, "The umbrella opened without any problem, just before it started to rain, but it failed to keep me dry unless I kept it perfectly level. Every time I bent over slightly I got soaked with water."

The salesperson opened the umbrella. It opened without any problem. He inspected the fabric next. It was a top-of-the-line, water-resistant material and had no holes. The inside of the umbrella, however, was as soaked as the customer. Why did Joe get soaked even though the umbrella was in perfect shape?

2. Jack's mom told him to stop counting stars and get in the car. The sun was blazing hot, and the family still had several miles to drive before reaching their cousins in Los Angeles. How could Jack see the stars in the middle of the day?

Caught in the Middle

GENIUS GENUS: WORD WIZARD

Many words and phrases have beginnings and endings in common. In the list below, find the word that belongs in the middle column for each row. The words must work as the ending to the word on the left and as the beginning to the word on the right. For example, with the words "ARROW" and "BOARD," we placed "HEAD" in the middle and created ARROW**HEAD** and **HEAD**BOARD.

I wonder if you will find the missing words here by trial-and-error or through insight ... Both will work! Good luck!

ARROW	HEAD	BOARD

COOK		CASE
SALT		FALL
BIRD		ROBE
BUTTER		SWATTER
MOON		BULB
HOT		HOUSE
FOOT		ROOM
PINE		SAUCE
QUARTER		ACHE
FRIEND		WRECK
PIN		CHAIR

GENIUS GENUS: SPATIAL SUPERSTAR

3-D Head-Scratcher

Using 15 additional lines, the same length as those used to the right, turn this 3-D box into four 3-D boxes. The boxes may be right against one another but may not overlap.

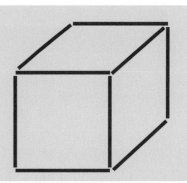

Congratulations! You've made it so far! I guess I can't call you "student" anymore—what should your new title be? Could it be ... Mastermind?

Color Guide

If you remember the colors of the rainbow in order (see p. 140), then decoding this message will be a cinch!

D O E T R E L Y R
R O I M H O E I B
R F A E R
O R N T E
O R U W C O
O M D O B S E
H N

___ ___ _____ ___ ___

_____ ___ _____

___ ____ _____ ?

Missing Number

What is the missing number?

4	2	3	4
3	2	?	1
5	1	2	5
1	8	1	3

GENIUS GENUS: LOGICAL LEADER

Broken Messages

Someone shook the box below so hard that the message inside broke apart.
At least we know the sequence of numbers below is the key to putting the words in order.
Can you determine the message?

3 4 7 6 2 5 7 4 3 4 2 4 4

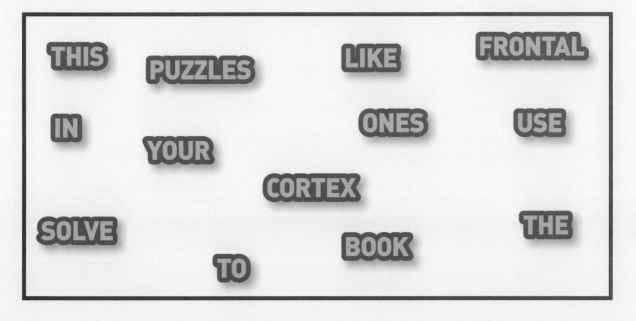

THIS   PUZZLES   LIKE   FRONTAL

IN   ONES   USE

YOUR

CORTEX

SOLVE   THE

BOOK

TO

Test Your S.M.A.R.T.S.!

(SUPERIOR MENTAL ACUITY AND RATIONALITY TESTING SYSTEM)

YOU'VE FINALLY MADE IT ... THIS IS THE FINAL CHALLENGE OF THE BOOK! OR IS IT? (MUAHAHA!)

Answer these four quiz questions, and then your big, beautiful brain will finally be mine, all MINE!

Oops, I got a little excited there. Forget I said that, OK? Focus all the power of your superior skull on my last tricky test (and if you're not mentally exhausted—try the bonus puzzle, too!)

1. When your brain tests possible solutions to a problem one by one, it's called _____ problem solving.

R random

S trial-and-error

E multistep

R time-and-again

Hidden Word: ___ ___ ___ ___ ___

$x + y = ?$

2. When your brain tests possible solutions to a problem all at once, it's called _____ problem solving.

E insight

T synchronous

T trial-and-error

S multi-solution

Hidden Word: ____ ____ ____ ____

3. Scientists found that watching _____ videos made people better at insight problem solving.

Z scary

N educational

Y funny

A cat

Hidden Word: ____ ____ ____ ____ ____

4. Watson the computer made history when he beat a human at _____.

E tennis

B chess

A Monopoly

T *Jeopardy!*

Hidden Word: ____ ____ ____ ____

RECORD YOUR ANSWERS HERE

1 2 3 4

YOU ARE HERE

Mastermind

M.S.B. (Mentally Superior Being)

Genuine genius

Watch out! Walking encyclopedia coming through

Budding egghead

You're pretty intelligent ... for a primate

Bet you can outwit Atom

Slightly smarter than you were an hour ago

Not a total blockhead

MASTERMIND METER

Congratulations, Mastermind!

If you've made it through the whole book, you have completed your transformation from puny-minded pupil to sharp super brain. So now I'll let you in on a little secret: You have passed the test to join E.V.I.L.— the Extraordinarily Villainous Intelligence League!

What's that? You actually thought I was investing all my time and energy just to make you smarter for your own good? HA! No way! I'm E.V.I.L.'s head recruiter. And YOU were the final piece of the puzzle.

By harnessing your beefed-up mental muscle, we E.V.I.L. geniuses will now have enough brainpower to make all those bitty blockheads of planet Earth do our bidding! With your super skull in our group, we can finally take over the world!

So say goodbye to your friends and loved ones ... because you're one of us now. Unless, of course, you solve this ultimate puzzle and take the pledge of our counter-organization: G.O.O.D.—Geniuses of Outstanding Decency.

To solve this puzzle, you need to have figured out my trick.
Here is your one and only clue:

When all seems bleak,
And you know not of what we speak,
For the answers you seek,
The chapter quizzes shall you peek.

| CH3 Q3 | | | CH7 Q1 | | | , |

| CH6 Q4 | CH3 Q2 | CH4 Q4 | CH6 Q1 | CH7 Q4 | CH5 Q2 | CH3 Q3 | CH9 Q2 | CH5 Q1 |

| CH8 Q1 | CH2 Q4 | CH6 Q2 | CH9 Q4 | CH8 Q4 | CH6 Q3 | CH4 Q3 | CH7 Q4 | CH3 Q4 | CH5 Q1 | , |

| CH7 Q3 | CH4 Q2 | CH7 Q2 | | CH6 Q1 | CH2 Q2 | | CH4 Q1 | CH9 Q1 | CH2 Q3 |

| CH8 Q1 | CH3 Q1 | | CH8 Q2 | CH8 Q3 | CH3 Q4 | CH3 Q3 | CH4 Q1 | CH6 Q2 |

| CH2 Q2 | CH3 Q4 | CH2 Q1 | CH9 Q3 | | CH5 Q4 | CH4 Q2 | CH4 Q4 |

| CH8 Q2 | CH4 Q2 | CH2 Q2 | CH5 Q1 | | CH3 Q4 | CH2 Q2 | CH9 Q4 | . |

| CH8 Q4 | CH5 Q3 | CH7 Q4 | CH2 Q1 |

(CH = chapter, Q = question)

SOLUTION: If you realized the code above could be broken by checking out the answers to the chapter quizzes, you should have figured out that this says:

I, A CERTIFIED MASTERMIND, VOW TO USE MY GENIUS ONLY FOR GOOD, NOT EVIL.

Certificate of Mental Achievement

BY THE POWERS VESTED IN US, THE

GENIUSES OF OUTSTANDING DECENCY (G.O.O.D.)

DO HEREBY VERIFY THAT

_____

(Your name here)

has successfully completed the mental tests and puzzles necessary
to earn the title of

CERTIFIED MASTERMIND

And that from _____ (today's date) forward, this Mastermind
hereby solemnly swears to uphold the principles of G.O.O.D. and to devote his
or her exceptional intelligence to serve the causes of justice and righteousness.
And, furthermore, to drive that no-good E.V.I.L. from planet Earth once and for all!

Argh! I spent this entire book making you a brainiac ... and all my hard work backfired!

I've taught you too well. You've outsmarted me this time, Mastermind ... but we've only scratched the surface.

You may be a certified Mastermind, but you're just getting to know the true power of your brain. I, on the other hand, have been training my thinker for years. And be warned: When we meet again, I'll be holding nothing back.

Let's see how you fare when you go noggin-to-noggin against the full strength of my exceptional egghead. It will be a G.O.O.D. vs. E.V.I.L. smarty-pants showdown ... and you're sure to lose!

Mark my words—I'll use your Mastermind for E.V.I.L. if it's the last thing I do.

Ima Genius

Ima Genius
Head Recruiter, E.V.I.L.

CHAPTER 2

Brain Maze, p. 18

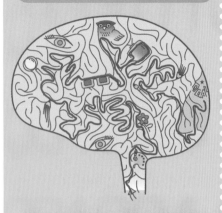

Cryptogram, p. 22

The giant squid has the largest eye of all animals

Eye Maze, p. 23

Color Blind, p. 26

Dog Vision, p. 27

1. fire hydrant 2. red pail 3. beach ball 4. basketball 5. flowerpot 6. cardinal 7. bunch of balloons 8. flags 9. red starfish 10. blue sand pail

Word Ladder, p. 29

B	R	A	I	N
T	R	A	I	N
T	R	A	I	L
T	R	A	W	L
C	R	A	W	L

Quiz, pp. 34-35

1. Translate light entering your eye into the electrical signals that the brain can understand 2. 2 3. polarized 4. Recognize faces

Hidden Words: 1. Look 2. Spot 3. Prey 4. Face

Eye See, p. 33

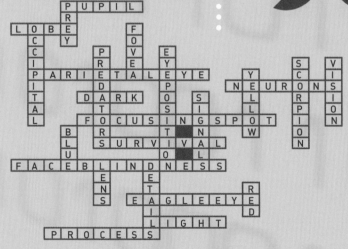

Flower Power, p. 30

You should see a flower magically appear in the empty box on the right. This is called an afterimage. When you stare at the white flower on the blue background, the parts of your eye that sense those colors get tired. When you switch your gaze to the blank box, other parts of your eye that sense the other colors try to make up for this. They create the illusion of the oddly colored flower.

Tricky Lines, p. 31

The lines are all the same length.

What Is It?, p. 31

If you are like most people, you saw three different images.
Image 1: an ice-cream cone or a dirty golf ball on a tee Image 2: a duck or bird's head Image 3: a boy wearing a cone-shaped hat

Illusive X, p. 32

CHAPTER 3

Brain Maze, p. 36

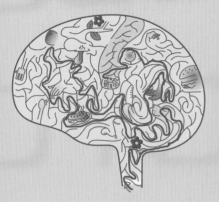

Sudoku Smells, p. 39

Cryptogram, p. 40

Your back is your least sensitive body part

Nose Maze, p. 41

Migration Mess, p. 44

Red Bird - Oregon • Orange Bird - Texas • Blue Bird - New Mexico • Green Bird - New York

License Plates, p. 48

FUN-G-4M - Tongue Doctor
MY-GR8 - Bird Lover
O-DOOR - Garbage Collector
HMN-Q-LS - Brain Doctor

Braille Code, p. 50

RAISED DOTS (BRAILLE) CAN BE FOUND ON ELEVATOR BUTTONS. CLOSE YOUR EYES TO TEST HOW SENSITIVE YOUR FINGERS ARE.

Find Your Way, p. 45

Bonus Answer: COMPASS

Touchy Topic, p. 51

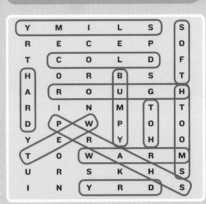

RECEPTORS IN YOUR SKIN

Quiz, pp. 52-53

1. The part of your brain that receives messages from your sense organs, like your eyes, ears, mouth, and nose
2. Someone who is extra sensitive to tastes—especially bitter tastes
3. migrate 4. synesthesia

Hidden Words: 1. Eyes 2. Eats 3. Bird 4. Note

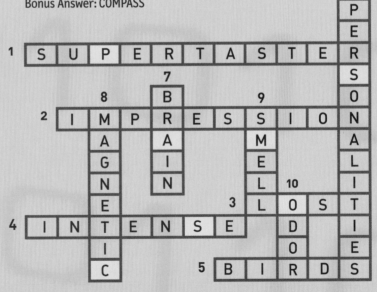

QUIZ AND PUZZLE ANSWERS

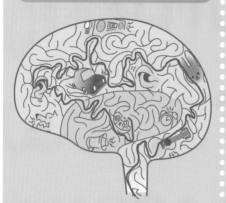
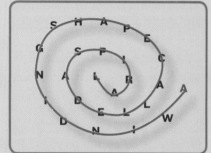

Though they are weak of sight,
Bats are masters of the night.

With their high-pitched clicks,
Which bounce off objects,
from beetles to bricks,

They send out an ultrasonic sound,
So delicious insects can be found.

Imagine having to avoid starvation,
If you had to use human echolocation!

ULTRASONIC HEARING

chainsaw - 110 • hair dryer - 70 • jet - 140 • whisper - 30 • lawn mower - 85-90 • refrigerator - 45 • firecracker - 130–150 • motorcycle - 88 • orchestra - 110 • tractor - 98

In your ear!

A baby's cry is louder than a car horn!

CRICKETS USE THEIR LEGS TO SENSE SOUND WAVES

1. Hair cells
2. Bats, dolphins
3. Stay away from its predator: bats
4. perfect pitch

Hidden Words: 1. Turn 2. Echo 3. Moth 4. Hear

CHAPTER 5
Brain Maze, p. 72

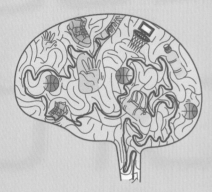

Cryptogram, p. 76

A baby horse can walk within an hour after birth

Spine Maze, p. 77

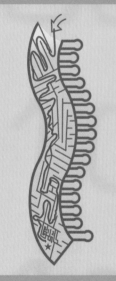

Jumpers, p. 80

RABBIT, HORSE, FLEA, IMPALA, DOLPHIN, TREE FROG, GRASSHOPPER, JUMPING SPIDER

ANSWER: LEAPFROG

Herculean Task, p. 81

Each beetle should carry a leg of the table, thereby carrying the entire table with everything on it!

Dog-Gone Smart, p. 83

You will need to remove at least one backpack to create an even distribution of 40 pounds on each side of the canoe. Although a few combinations will work, the simplest solution is to remove Mitsi's backpack and create the following groups:

Jack with backpack (13 + 1) + Kei-Ko with backpack (18 + 5) + Mitsi's backpack (3) = 40 pounds

Max with backpack (25 + 3) + Gazer with backpack (6 + 2) + Mitsi (4) = 40 pounds

Letter Swap, p. 87

W	E	D	O	N	T	J	U	S	T	G	E	T	S
E	N	S	A	T	I	O	N	S	F	R	O	M	O
U	R	A	R	M	S	A	N	D	L	E	G	S	.
O	U	R	I	N	T	E	R	N	A	L	O	R	G
A	N	S	C	A	N	S	E	N	D	T	H	E	M
T	O	O	.	H	U	N	G	E	R	P	A	I	N
S	L	E	T	Y	O	U	K	N	O	W	I	T	I
S	T	I	M	E	T	O	E	A	T	!			

WE DON'T JUST GET SENSATIONS FROM OUR ARMS AND LEGS. OUR INTERNAL ORGANS CAN SEND THEM TOO. HUNGER PANGS LET YOU KNOW IT IS TIME TO EAT!

Hidden Truth, p. 87

	1	2	3	4	5	6	7	8	9	10
	C	S	C	N	E	H	N	S	P	K
	G	I	O	D	M	R	K	I	K	I
	R	O	C	H	M	B	G	B	O	S
	E	O	R	E	H	A	K	M	D	M
	I	R	I	S	D	M	U	D	M	K

GOOSEBUMPS

It's All Related, p. 86

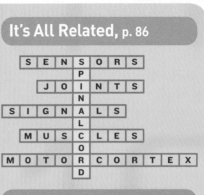

Quiz, pp. 88–89

1. all of the above 2. Cheetah
3. a robotic arm 4. balance

Hidden Words: 1. Bids 2. Fast 3. Move 4. Feel

QUIZ AND PUZZLE ANSWERS

CHAPTER 6

Brain Maze, p. 90

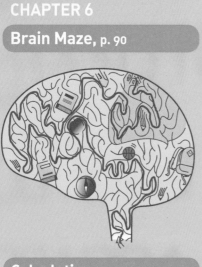

Calculating, p. 93

If you flip a calculator upside down, several of the numbers can be read as letters. When you read these numbers upside down, they spell out:

ZOE SELLS EEL ShOES

Cryptogram, p. 94

Listening to music boosts spatial reasoning

Neuron Maze, p. 95

Driving You Nuts, p. 98

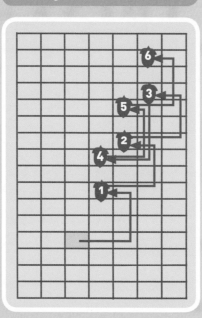

Cube Confusion, p. 99

Fragile Package, p. 102

Run Around, p. 103

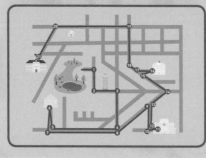

Including backtracking after dropping off deliveries on one-way streets, the total number of turns you make using this route is 21. If your route uses fewer turns, then you get a promotion to delivery supervisor!

Intersections, p. 104

D

Number Transformation, p. 104

18 → 45

Crazy Maze, p. 105

C

Shape Shift, p. 105

Quiz, pp. 106–107

1. parietal cortex and hippocampus
2. ignore everything on his left side
3. Their whiskers 4. Trunk Packers, Navigators

Hidden Words: 1. Part 2. Side 3. Dark 4. Pack

CHAPTER 7

Brain Maze, p. 108

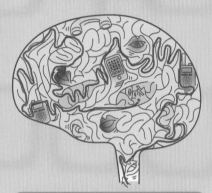

Crossed Words, p. 111

B	R	A	I	N
A	O	R	T	A
S	L	E	E	P
S	L	A	M	S

Cryptogram, p. 112

It is impossible to sing with an accent!

Question Mark Maze, p. 113

Bubble Trouble, p. 116

STOP BLOWING BUBBLES IN YOUR WATER!

Spreading the Word, p. 117

The message reaches all of Colony A first since the messenger is in the center of the colony. By the second round of communication (in green), the message has already reached more termites in Colony A. The farther from the center the messenger is, the longer it will take the message to reach the entire colony. Colony B needs two more "rounds" than Colony A for the message to spread to everyone.

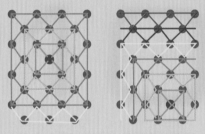

Bee Dance, p. 117

The colony will follow Clara Bee because her dance included all of the necessary information about the direction and distance they'll need to find the nectar. The other dances didn't tell about *both* direction and distance.

Body Lingo, p. 121

1. Defensive 2. Lost in Thought
3. Nervous 4. Interested 5. Bored
6. Confident 7. Ready 8. Doubtful
9. Not Confident 10. Truthful

Out of the Box, p. 121

1. They are at a playground, and the kids want to play on the seesaw.
2. The friend is playing Monopoly.
3. They are building a city out of building blocks.

Deceptive Design, p. 122

If you look closely, you will see the word "FIND" built into the banister.

Word Chain, p. 122

NEIGHBORELATIVELEPHANTABLETO-PLAYROOMACARONILLUSION

Coordinated, p. 123

In the language Afrikaans, bees go "zoem, zoem"

	1	2	3	4	5	6	7	8
a	I	N	T	H	E	L	A	N
b	G	U	A	G	E	A	F	R
c	I	K	A	A	N	S	,	B
d	E	E	S	G	O	"	Z	O
e	E	M	,	Z	O	E	M	"

Mess of a Story, pp. 123

While driving and looking for the LAUNDROMAT, we saw a large STEAM SHOVEL flipped over on its side, trapping the driver. A POLICEWOMAN came over to help, but too many PEDESTRIANS were in the way. The PARAMEDICS got there in plenty of time to take the driver to the HOSPITAL.

Quiz, pp. 124-125

1. speak or write words 2. listen to and understand words 3. Directions to find food 4. corpus callosum

Hidden Words: 1. Area 2. Word 3. Hive 4. Join

CHAPTER 8

Brain Maze, p. 126

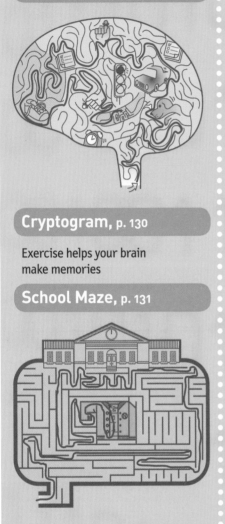

Cryptogram, p. 130

Exercise helps your brain make memories

School Maze, p. 131

Backtracking, p. 133

One hour. The trek from the top of the mountain back to her house took four hours without any delays. Since the path and pace were the same in both directions, the trek to the top of the mountain should have taken four hours as well, but it took six. The extra two hours were spent finding the water bottle and returning. That means Sally spent one hour finding the bottle and one hour returning to the point on the path where she had turned back to find the bottle.

It's in the Details, pp. 134-135

Aha, we tricked you! Those questions cannot be answered by the story. None of the details were provided, but we inserted language into the story to help your brain make some memories based on what you had read. Also, by setting this activity up as a puzzle and asking you questions in a way that suggested there were correct answers, we made your mind provide details that weren't given in the story. Pretty tricky, right? OK, a bit mean, too, perhaps, but at least now you see how your memory cannot always be trusted.

Face It, p. 138

There are no right or wrong answers when it comes to memory and association. Whatever words or order work for you IS the answer.

It's a Jumble, pp. 139, 141

BIKE, RAKE, HEIGHT, HIKE, BAKE, RIGHT

Locker Layout, p. 139, 141

Missing items: umbrella, green book, guinea pig, hairbrush, flower, coat hook

Quiz, pp. 142–143

1. Short-term memories
2. By strengthening connections between neurons 3. anterograde amnesia 4. can't forget anything

Hidden Words: 1. Term 2. Give 3. Make 4. Keep

CHAPTER 9

Brain Maze, p. 144

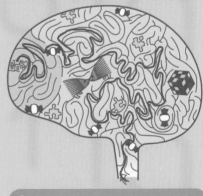

Cryptogram, p. 148

Sleeping can help your brain solve problems

Box Maze, p. 149

Word Camo, p. 152

Tomato Adrift

When the limo used for transporting the president was seen hauling a magnetic rowboat to the pier, reporters became suspicious. This was no way to chase aliens who had stolen the president's bronze bracelet. Perhaps the military would forgo attacking the aliens. After all, they looked like tomatoes and the president had fed them a subpar rotisserie chicken in tomato sauce, boathouse almonds, and broccoli onboard her yacht. And that is no way to treat guests; especially those who smell amazing even after bathing in tapioca melon pudding. What's next ... marzipan therapy?

Beastly Phrases, p. 153

1. Birdbrain 2. Black Sheep in the Family
3. Horse Sense 4. A Leopard Can't Change Its Spots

Codebreaker, p. 155

The code uses the position of letters in the alphabet, so A = 1, B = 2 ... Z = 26. The hint "PUZZLE" provided the best clue given that there are 26 letters in the alphabet and the letter "Z" was represented by "26."

9	13	1		7	5	14	9	21	19
I	M	A		G	E	N	I	U	S

Letter Logic, p. 156

Y	O	U	R		B	R	A	I	N		I	S		T	H	E
O	N	L	Y		O	R	G	A	N		T	H	A	T		
C	A	N	N	O	T		F	E	E	L		P	A	I	N	.

Tricky Riddles, p. 156

1. Joe opened the umbrella but was holding it upside down, allowing it to fill with water and create a miniature waterfall every time he tipped it! 2. The stars Jack was counting were the movie stars passing by in Hollywood. They can often be seen during the day shopping or going to lunch.

Caught in the Middle, p. 157

ARROW	HEAD	BOARD
COOK	BOOK	CASE
SALT	WATER	FALL
BIRD	BATH	ROBE
BUTTER	FLY	SWATTER
MOON	LIGHT	BULB
HOT	DOG	HOUSE
FOOT	BALL (or BATH)	ROOM
PINE	APPLE	SAUCE
QUARTER	BACK	ACHE
FRIEND	SHIP	WRECK
PIN	WHEEL	CHAIR

3-D Head-Scratcher, p. 157

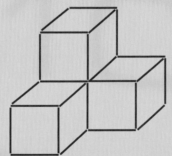

You actually only need to draw two boxes beside the first. The fourth box is implied, as it is not seen but is needed to support the highest box.

Color Guide, p. 158

Group the letters in the order of the rainbow, ROY G. BIV, and then unscramble the letters in each color group to form words. You will see a message when you place the words in the order of colors in the rainbow.

DOYOUREMEMBERTHEORDEROFCOLORSINTHERAINBOW

Missing Number, p. 159

The missing number is 7. If you add the numbers of individual columns or rows, the total will equal 13.

Broken Messages, p. 159

The number sequence stands for the number of letters in each word. Start with the words that are obvious. The word "cortex" is the only six-letter word, and the word "solve" is the only five-letter word. If you move on to the seven-letter words next, you have a choice of "frontal" and "puzzles," and only the word "frontal" fits in front of the word "cortex." If you continue using logic and trial-and-error, you will discover the message:

USE YOUR FRONTAL CORTEX TO SOLVE PUZZLES LIKE THE ONES IN THIS BOOK

Quiz, pp. 160–161

1. trial-and-error 2. insight
3. funny 4. *Jeopardy!*

Hidden Words: 1. Errs 2. Test 3. Zany
4. Beat

Index

Illustration Credits

DRMS: Dreamstime; GI: Getty Images; IS: iStockphoto; SS: Shutterstock

Front cover (BACK), Arenacreative/DRMS; (UP RT), Valkos/DRMS; (UP CTR), Svitlana-ua/SS; (CTR LE), Sashkin/SS; (CTR LE BACK), Ckarxz/DRMS; (CTR RT), DNY59/IS; (LO LE) Klaus Hackenberg/Corbis; (LO RT), Damedeeso/DRMS **back cover** (UP LE), Kevin Rechin; (UP RT), Alhovik/SS; (CTR LE), Tharakorn Arunothai/SS; (CTR), Kevin Rechin; (LO LE), Mega Pixel/SS

Front matter 1 (LE & RT), Kevin Rechin; 1 (Background), Arenacreative/DRMS; 3 (CTR RT), DNY59/IS; 3 (LOLE), Ckarxz/DRMS; 4 (UP CTR), Valkos/DRMS; 4 (UP RT), Svitlana-ua/SS; 4 (LO), PeterVrabel/SS; 5 (LO), Damedeeso/DRMS; 6 (UP), Shevs/SS; 6 (LE), Kevin Rechin; 6 (LO), Sashkin/SS; 7 (UP CTR), Tharakorn Arunothai/SS; 7 (RT), Kevin Rechin; 8 (UP RT), Mega Pixel/SS; 8 (LO RT), Vitaly Korovin **Chapter 1** 10 (LO LE), GeorgiosArt/IS; 10 (LO CTR LE), Ken Brown/IS; 10 (LO CTR), stocksnapper/IS; 10 (LO CTR RT), pictore/IS; 10 (LO RT), Tiger Images/IS; 11 (UP), Sofia Santos/IS; 11 (RT), erashov/IS; 11 (LO), Kirill__M/SS; 12–13 (UP), Matjaz Preseren/SS; 12 (CTR LE), GeorgiosArt/IS; 12 (CTR RT), Ken Brown/IS; 12 (LO LE), R. Gino Santa Maria/SS; 12 (LO RT), Alhovik/SS; 13 (CTR), stocksnapper/IS; 13 (CTR RT), pictore/IS; 13 (LO LE), slpix/SS; 13 (LO RT), Africa Studio/SS; 14 (LE), RAJ CREATIONZS/SS; 14 (LO RT), maggee/SS; 14–15 (UP), Leigh Prather/SS; 15 (CTR RT), Matjaz Preseren/SS; 15 (LO RT), pixologicstudio/IS; 16 (UP LE), Julien Tromeur/SS; 16 (RT), Danny E Hooks/SS; 16 (LO), George Karbus Photography/cultura/Corbis; 17 (LO), PathDoc/SS; 17 (binary code), winui/SS; 17 (piggy bank), aslysun/SS; 17 (camera), Masalski Maksim/SS; 17 (guitar), AlexMaster/SS; 17 (brain), Nerthuz/SS; 17 (girl), Hans Kim/SS; 17 (microscope), Sashkin/SS; 17 (paints), Svitlana-ua/SS; 17 (Rubik's cube), PeterVrabel/SS **Chapter 2** 18 (LO), Junichi Tsuneoka; 19 (UP RT), Pete Pahham/SS; 20 (CTR LE), Tuomas Kujansuu/IS; 20 (CTR RT), janulla/IS; 20 (LO), Alexilus/SS; 21 (UP RT), jaroon/IS; 21 (LO LE), age fotostock/Alamy; 21 (LO RT), jimmyjamesbond/IS; 22 (UP), Garsya/SS; 23, Junichi Tsuneoka; 24 (LO LE), GlobalP/IS; 25 (UP LE), Kim Taylor/Nature Picture Library; 25 (CTR LE), Konstantin Nechaev/Alamy; 25 (CTR RT), Ingo Arndt/Minden Pictures; 25 (LO RT), natuska/SS; 27 (playground), Everything/SS; 27 (fire hydrant), NikkosDaskalakis/IS; 27 (sand and toys), Ivonne Wierink/SS; 27 (boy), michaeljung/SS; 27 (balloons), artjazz/SS; 27 (bucket of toys), lkphotographers/SS; 27 (flowers), Africa Studio/SS; 27 (basketball), Lightspring/SS; 27 (cardinal), chas53/IS; 27 (flags), Dmytro_Skorobogatov/IS; 27 (beach ball), Stepan Bormotov/SS; 28 (CTR LE), baibaz/SS; 28 (LO RT), catnap72/IS; 28 (LO CTR), jaroon/IS; 28 (LO RT inset), snapphoto/IS; 29 (CTR RT), Lisa S./SS; 29 (LO LE), Rawpixel/SS; 30 (UP RT), Kevin Rechin; 32 (UP), GlobalStock/IS; 33 (RT), Pete Pahham/SS; 34 (LO RT), billyhoiler/IS; 35 (UP LE), sekarb/IS **Chapter 3** 36 (UP RT), exopixel/SS; 36 (LO), Junichi Tsuneoka; 37 (UP LE), Spasta/SS; 37 (CTR RT), Cathleen A Clapper/SS; 38 (UP CTR), The Natural History Museum/Trustees of the Natural History Museum, London; 38 (CTR RT), Aaron Amat/SS; 38 (LO), SergiyN/SS; 39 (banana), brulove/SS; 39 (rose), topseller/SS; 39 (orange), Maks Narodenko/SS; 39 (lemon), svetok30/SS; 39 (onion), Hong Vo/SS; 39 (mint), Dionisvera/SS; 39 (LO LE), Anna Hoychuk/SS; 39 (LO RT), kgphoto/IS; 41, Junichi Tsuneoka; 42 (LO), Duston Todd/Rubberball/Corbis; 43 (UP RT), Smit/SS; 43 (LE), Butterfly Hunter/SS; 43 (LO RT), Kalin Eftimov/SS; 44 (UP), Eric Isselee/SS; 45 (UP RT), Francesco Ocello/SS; 46 (UP RT), nikkytok/SS; 46 (CTR LE), Vorobyeva/SS; 46 (LO CTR), Bryan Solomon/IS; 46 (LO RT), Margorius/SS; 47 (LO RT), Patrick Foto/SS; 48 (UP), Mega Pixel/SS; 48 (LO LE), Sari ONeal/SS; 48 (LO CTR LE), bikeriderlondon/SS; 48 (LO CTR RT), Sebastian Kaulitzki/SS; 48 (LO RT), Jaimie Duplass/SS; 49 (UP LE), slobo/IS; 49 (UP RT), DNY59/IS; 49 (CTR), Pictac/IS; 49 (LO RT), bonzodog/SS; 50 (UP LE), rvlsoft/SS; 52 (LO RT), Sebastian Kaulitzki/SS; 53 (UP CTR), Anna Kucherova/SS; 53 (CTR), Eric Isselee/SS **Chapter 4** 54 (UP RT), Mega Pixel/SS; 54 (LO), Junichi Tsuneoka; 55 (UP), Javier Brosch/SS; 56 (UP CTR), slobo/IS; 56 (LO), Alexilus/SS; 57 (LO LE), lisafx/IS; 57 (LO RT), Anan Kaewkhammul/SS; 59, Junichi Tsuneoka; 60 (UP), stokkete/IS; 60 (LO), hlansdown/IS; 61 (UP RT), Donhype/IS; 61 (LE), Edo Schmidt/Alamy; 61 (LO RT), Francisco Martinez-Clavel Martinez/Alamy; 62 (LO CTR), Craig Dingle/IS; 64 (UP RT), Keith Publicover/SS; 64–65 (LO), Lars Baron/GI; 65 (UP RT), Modestil/SS; 65 (CTR RT), Keith Publicover/SS; 65 (LO RT), imac/IS; 66 (LE), GlobalP/IS; 67 (hair dryer), rgbdigital/IS; 67 (tractor), kamski/IS; 67 (chainsaw), kamil/IS; 67 (jet), RobHowarth/IS; 67 (refrigerator), Todd Taulman/DRMS; 67 (whisper), digitalskillet/IS; 67 (firecracker), PapaBear/IS; 67 (motorcycle), Robert Churchill/IS; 67 (lawn mower), Hurst Photo/SS; 67 (orchestra), Bastiaan Slabbers/IS; 68 (basset hound), GlobalP/IS; 68 (polar bear), Frank Hildebrand/IS; 68 (hippo), pjmalsbury/IS; 68 (rabbit), Oktay Ortakcioglu/IS; 68 (German shepherd), Nikolai Tsvetkov/IS; 68 (lynx), GlobalP/IS; 68 (fox), nattanan726/IS; 68 (elephant), NightOwlZA/IS; 70 (LO RT), Henrik5000/IS; 71 (CTR), Francisco Martinez-Clavel Martinez/Alamy **Chapter 5** 72 (UP RT), naluwan/SS; 72 (LO), Junichi Tsuneoka; 73 (UP RT), Lightspring/SS; 74 (CTR LE), CREATISTA/SS; 74 (CTR RT), VLADGRIN/SS; 74–75, Jiang Dao Hua/SS; 75 (LO), sdominick/IS; 77 (CTR), Junichi Tsuneoka; 77 (CTR RT), Sebastian Kaulitzki/SS; 78 (UP RT), Chones/SS; 78 (LO), Gregory Wilson/National Geographic Creative; 79 (UP RT), dennisvdw/IS; 79 (CTR LE), Stephen Gaunt/Focus Images Ltd; 79 (CTR RT), Cosmin Manci/SS; 79 (LO RT), Mauricio Handler/National Geographic Creative; 80 (RT), Erik Isakson/RubberBall/Alamy; 81 (bucket), Pashalgnatov/IS; 81 (table), photka/SS; 81 (leaves), Kichigin/SS; 81 (turkey), AdShooter/IS; 81 (wood), Difydave/IS; 81 (apples), Chris_Elwell/IS; 81 (tree), Shebeko/SS; 81 (cake), gmnicholas/IS; 81 (beetles), Cosmin Manci/SS; 82 (UP), Vladislav Ociacia/IS; 82 (CTR LE), 3alexd/IS; 82 (LO RT), Tim UR/SS; 82 (LO RT), siscosoler/IS; 83 (UP LE), irin-k/SS; 83 (UP RT), Kevin C. Cox/GI; 83 (CTR LE), MarkCoffeyPhoto/IS; 83 (CTR RT), MarkCoffeyPhoto/IS; 83 (LO LE), walik/IS; 83 (LO CTR), WilleeCole/IS; 83 (LO RT), walik/IS; 84 (LO RT), Ollyy/SS; 85 (UP RT), 4x6/IS; 85 (LO ALL), Becky Hale/NGS; 87 (UP RT), Tharakorn Arunothai/SS; 88 (LO), Judith Glick Ehrenthal/IS; 89 (UP LE), Winai Tepsuttinun/SS; 89 (CTR), flavijus/IS **Chapter 6** 90 (UP RT), Garsya/SS; 90 (LO), Junichi Tsuneoka; 91 (UP RT), ra2studio/SS; 92 (UP LE), IPGGutenbergUKLtd/IS; 92 (LO), Jamie Roach/SS; 93 (UP LE), itographer/IS; 93 (CTR), Christopher Futcher/IS; 93 (LO RT), chonrawit boonprakob/SS; 95 (LE), Junichi Tsuneoka; 95 (RT), Sebastian Kaulitzki/SS; 96 (LO), Martyn Vickery/Alamy; 97 (UP), Kevin Wheal/Alamy; 97 (UP RT), stocker1970/SS; 97 (CTR RT), Tim Ayers/Alamy; 97 (LO LE), GP232/IS; 97 (LO RT), anankkml/IS; 98 (acorns), nevodka/IS; 98 (LO), IrinaK/SS; 100 (LE), miljko/IS; 100 (LO RT), 1MoreCreative/IS; 100 (LO RT inset), Tsekhmister/SS; 101 (CTR LE), mingusen/IS; 101 (CTR RT), Harry Stewart/Alamy; 101 (LO), tomograf/IS; 101 (LO inset), insima/SS; 102 (UP RT), Mike Flippo/SS; 106 (LO), Willard/IS; 107 (CTR), Oktay Ortakcioglu/IS; 107 (LO RT), Svitlana-ua/SS **Chapter 7** 108 (UP RT), rangizzz/SS; 108 (LO), Junichi Tsuneoka; 109 (LE), Dayna More/SS; 110 (UP RT), aastoc/SS; 110 (LO), anatols/IS; 111 (LO), Inna Astakhova/SS; 113, Junichi Tsuneoka; 114 (CTR RT), Ingo Arndt/Minden Pictures; 114 (LO), Lucarelli Temistocle/SS; 115 (CTR RT), Tsekhmister/SS; 115 (LO LE), ALesik/IS; 115 (UP RT), George Grall/ National Geographic Creative; 116 (RT), Pannochka/SS; 117 (termites), Ingo Arndt/Minden Pictures; 117 (LO RT), arlindo71/IS; 118 (LO), RuslanDashinsky/IS; 119 (UP RT), astudio/IS; 119 (LO LE), shayes17/IS; 119 (LO RT), welzevoul/SS; 121 (1), drbimages/IS; 121 (2), drbimages/IS; 121 (3), PeskyMonkey/IS; 121 (4), Huchen Lu/IS; 121 (5), Ollyy/SS; 121 (6), Dean Drobot/SS; 121 (7), Aldo Murillo/IS; 121 (8), EHStock/IS; 121 (9), Lars Zahner/SS; 121 (10), Chris from Paris/SS; 122 (LO), Picsfive/SS; 123 (RT), damedeeso/IS; 124 (LO RT), Ingo Arndt/Minden Pictures; 125 (CTR), arlindo71/IS **Chapter 8** 126 (UP RT), drbimages/IS; 126 (LO), Junichi Tsuneoka; 127 (RT), Quasarphoto/IS; 128 (UP), koosen/SS; 128 (CTR), Erik Khalitov/IS; 128 (LO), jozsef73/IS; 129 (UP), bloodua/IS; 129 (CTR), Lisa Thornberg/IS; 129 (LO), NatUlrich/SS; 131, Junichi Tsuneoka; 132 (UP RT), Cheryl E. Davis/SS; 132 (LE), monkeybusinessimages/IS; 132 (LO RT), Robyn Mackenzie/SS; 133 (CTR LE), Abel Tumik/SS; 133 (LO RT), Max Topchii/SS; 134 (UP), gbh007/IS; 136 (LE), stockphoto mania/SS; 136 (RT), Hurst Photo/SS; 137 (UP LE), Walt Disney Co./courtesy Everett Collection; 137 (LO), Jirsak/SS; 138 (UP LE), Alan Bailey/SS; 138 (CTR LE), sashahaltam/SS; 138 (CTR RT), Dave Pot/SS; 138 (LO LE), drbimages/IS; 138 (LO CTR), 4x6/IS; 138 (LO RT), iko/SS; 139 (locker), stevezmina1/Digital Vision Vectors/GI; 139 (hat), ljpat/IS; 139 (guinea pig), MattStaples/IS; 139 (umbrella), wabeno/IS; 139 (books), blackred/IS; 139 (flowers), jurisam/IS; 139 (hairbrush), Africa Studio/SS; 139 (backpack), Pogonici/IS; 139 (hanger), chonrawit boonprakob/SS; 139 (boots), Sarycheva Olesia/SS; 140 (UP), Mary_L/SS; 140 (LE), Vorobyeva/SS; 140 (LO), Dan Kosmayer/SS; 141 (locker), stevezmina1/Digital Vision Vectors/GI; 141 (hat), ljpat/IS; 141 (ball), irin-k/SS; 141 (books), blackred/IS; 141 (flowers), jurisam/IS; 141 (backpack), Pogonici/IS; 141 (lunch bag), photka/IS; 141 (boots), Sarycheva Olesia/SS; 142 (LO), Hurst Photo/SS; 143 (CTR), Walt Disney Co./courtesy Everett Collection **Chapter 9** 144 (UP RT), manzrussali/SS; 144 (LO), Junichi Tsuneoka; 145 (UP), Ultrashock/SS; 146 (UP RT), ponsulak/SS; 146 (CTR LE), Nattika/SS; 146 (LO CTR), Africa Studio/SS; 146 (LO RT), kostudio/SS; 147 (UP RT), sd619/IS; 147 (CTR RT), stanley45/IS; 147 (LO LE), Erik Karits/SS; 149, Junichi Tsuneoka; 150 (UP RT), surabhi25/IS; 150 (LO LE), Tribalium/IS; 150 (LO RT), mj0007/IS; 151 (UP LE), Taalvi/IS; 151 (UP LE inset), yvdavyd/IS; 151 (CTR RT), Thomas Marent/Minden Pictures; 151 (LO RT), imageBROKER/Alamy; 152 (CTR LE), Dionisvera/SS; 152 (LO RT), Ilya Shulika/SS; 153 (rain), Vizerskaya/IS; 153 (horse), mari_art/IS; 153 (pennies), Eldad Carin/IS; 153 (sheep), Jan_Neville/IS; 153 (family), laflor/IS; 153 (can), Spauln/IS; 153 (coins), Eldad Carin/IS; 153 (leopard), GlobalP/IS; 153 (bird), Antagain/IS; 153 (bee), arlindo71/IS; 154 (CTR LE), AP Photo/Seth Wenig; 154 (LO LE), Lyudmyla Kharlamova/SS; 154 (LO RT), annt/SS; 155 (RT), NASA/JPL-Caltech; 155 (LO), greatideapl/IS; 158 (UP LE), Africa Studio/SS; 160 (LO), Photoprofi30/IS; 161 (UP), SS; 161 (CTR), BaLL LunLa/SS

For Grandpa Myrv, who taught me to ask why (and almost always knows the answer). -SWD

Copyright © 2015 National Geographic Society

Published by National Geographic Partners, LLC. All rights reserved. Reproduction of the whole or any part of the contents without written permission from the publisher is prohibited.

Staff for This Book
Becky Baines, *Project Editor*
Amanda Larsen, *Art Director*
John Foster, *Designer*
Lori Epstein, *Senior Photo Editor*
Annette Kiesow, *Photo Editor*
Paige Towler, *Editorial Assistant*
Sanjida Rashid and Rachel Kenny, *Design Production Assistants*
Tammi Colleary-Loach, *Rights Clearance Manager*
Grace Hill, *Managing Editor*
Mike O'Connor, *Production Editor*
Lewis R. Bassford, *Production Manager*
Rachel Faulise, *Manager, Production Services*
Susan Borke, *Legal and Business Affairs*

Puzzles designed by Julie K. Cohen, www.juliekcohen.com

Senior Management Team, Kids Publishing and Media
Nancy Laties Feresten, *Senior Vice President*; Jennifer Emmett, *Vice President, Editorial Director, Kids Books*; Julie Vosburgh Agnone, *Vice President, Editorial Operations*; Rachel Buchholz, *Editor and Vice President, NG Kids magazine*; Michelle Sullivan, *Vice President, Kids Digital*; Eva Absher-Schantz, *Design Director*; Jay Sumner, *Photo Director*; Hannah August, *Marketing Director*; R. Gary Colbert, *Production Director*

Digital Anne McCormack, *Director*; Laura Goertzel, Sara Zeglin, *Producers*; Emma Rigney, *Creative Producer*; Bianca Bowman, *Assistant Producer*; Natalie Jones, *Senior Product Manager*

Since 1888, the National Geographic Society has funded more than 12,000 research, exploration, and preservation projects around the world. The Society receives funds from National Geographic Partners, LLC, funded in part by your purchase. A portion of the proceeds from this book supports this vital work. To learn more, visit natgeo.com/info.

NATIONAL GEOGRAPHIC and Yellow Border Design are trademarks of the National Geographic Society, used under license.

For more information, please visit nationalgeographic.com, call 1-877-873-6846, or write to the following address:

National Geographic Partners
1145 17th Street N.W.
Washington, D.C. 20036-4688 U.S.A.

Visit us online at nationalgeographic.com/books

For librarians and teachers: ngchildrensbooks.org

More for kids from National Geographic: natgeokids.com

For information about special discounts for bulk purchases, please contact National Geographic Books Special Sales: specialsales@natgeo.com

For rights or permissions inquiries, please contact National Geographic Books Subsidiary Rights: bookrights@natgeo.com

ISBN: 978-1-4263-2110-8

Printed in China
20/RRDH/3